Grass Mountain

Grass Mountain

A Seven Day Intensive in Ch'an Training

with Master Nan Huai-Chin

translated by
Margaret Yuan (Liu Yu-hung)
&
Janis Walker

Samuel Weiser, Inc.
York Beach, Maine

First published in 1986 by
Samuel Weiser, Inc.
Box 612
York Beach, Maine 03910

ISBN 0-87728-612-4
Library of Congress Catalog Card Number: 85-50461

Cover photograph ©Harold Lundsted, 1983

Special thanks to Ch'ang Chi, who recorded the ch'an training
session.

Typeset in 10 point Schoolbook
Printed in the United States of America

Contents

About the Master

Ch'an Master Nan Huai-chin was born in 1918 to a scholar class family living in Luo Ch'ing in Chekiang Province. During his childhood he was tutored in the Chinese Classics, and by the age of seventeen had mastered the works of the Confucian and Taoist sages. As a youth, he studied the ancient arts of Chinese kung-fu, including swordsmanship. His studies also included literature, poetry, and calligraphy as essentials of a classical education among the upper classes, as well as herbal medicine and the *I Ching*.

He continuously sought out Taoist and Buddhist masters, and spent much of his time in old temples and the hermitages of these learned and deeply cultivated men. Much of the great knowledge he received is not written, but handed down in oral teaching direct from a master to his chosen disciples.

In the *Collection of the Wei Mo Hall** it is recorded that, in 1942, at the age of 24, Master Nan was a participant in a Ch'an training led by his master Yuan Huan Hsien. It was soon thereafter that he went up into the famous mountain temple on Mount O-Mei, which is one of the four most famous seats of Buddhist cultivation in China. He remained there in seclusion until 1945. During this time, he verified his experience against the teachings of the entire Buddhist canon.

In 1945, he left Mount O-Mei and traveled to Tibet to learn from the masters of the Esoteric School of Buddhism. The Hutuktu (Living Buddha) Kung Ka of the White Sect at last verified him as a master and gave him the official title of esoteric Master.

Collection of Wei Mo Hall, published in Chengtu, Szechuan, 1943.

From 1947-1969, he was sought out by many students. He was a teacher, lecturer, sometimes hermit, Professor of Philosophy at the College of Chinese Culture Graduate School in Taipei, and author. His first book, *The Sea of Zen*, was published in 1956. In 1969 he organized the East-West Essence Society. The new Society's first activity was a six-month course in Ch'an training.

From 1977 to 1979 the Master was in seclusion to concentrate on deepening his own practice. With the exception of these two years, he has led a Ch'an training each year since 1952 at the Chinese Lunar New Year. These trainings are often attended by more than 100 participants from all walks of life.

Acknowledgments

This book can be said to have begun in 1978. To this long preparation Master Nan and many people contributed their time, understanding and knowledge. We thank them all now for their help and support.

During the months of translation, we came to realize our great debt to all those translators – especially Charles Luk (Lu Kuan Yu) – who came before us whose work made ours so much easier. We thank them for their legacy with our deepest respect.

Whatever we may say in gratitude to Master Nan himself would never be enough. The quality of his humanness, his humor, his unfailing ability to show us a mirror of our true selves just by being his true self are all so extraordinary that we are at a loss to thank him in words. We offer this small book to him as a token of our true appreciation.

Introduction

What is Ch'an? What is Ch'an training? What is Ch'an teaching? Is Ch'an the same as the Japanese Zen, which many westerners are now familiar with due to the pioneering work of D. T. Suzuki and so many others?

This transcribed, day-by-day account of a Ch'an training held in Taiwan in 1962 holds the key to these and many more questions. We experience Ch'an through the minds and eyes of the participants, the interaction of Master and students. Through the human strivings of these individuals in a unique process, we find an insight into the essence of the Ch'an experience. This is not a scholarly exposition of principles, Sutras or history, but a living record of seven days in the lives of some thirty people. It is the first section to be translated of a longer work by Master Nan entitled *Profiles of Zen Training*.[1]

The center of this Ch'an training record is, of course, the Master. Professor Huai Chin Nan is himself a considerable force influencing contemporary Chinese culture. His books are standard university references on Confucian thought, and his many Buddhist and Taoist works are also highly regarded and widely read. His great contributions stem from tireless teaching, writing and practice. He combines great scholarship with the ability to apply and communicate his knowledge. This wholeness is rare in our age of over-particularization, and makes him one to whom the term Master may be properly applied.

The participants in this training are men and women of all ages and from all backgrounds. Some are successful

---

[1]This work is available in Chinese under the title *Hsi Ch'an Lu Yin*, published in Taipei in 1976. The work in its entirety is not yet available in English.

business people, military officers, students, housewives or professors. Some are Buddhist clergy. Some are beginners and some have many years of experience in meditation. Several of them are many years the Master's senior in age, and have now passed away. Several of the young people have gone on to become successful in many fields, and most are still among the Master's students today, and are seen at Ch'an trainings every year.

Certain things about Chinese Ch'an training may seem strange to those familiar with other systems of training, such as Japanese Zen or yogic practices. What may seem especially strange is the fact that the Master speaks during the periods of meditation. One must remember that Ch'an is above all a living pathway, a "gateless gate," an unlimited way, and it is in that great spirit of Ch'an that the Master speaks or remains silent. He is able to combine many methods from all of Buddhist tradition, as well as those deriving from Taoist or Confucian sources. These he blends into such a rich teaching that everyone, from beginners to old hands, always find something useful, inspiring and illuminating. Master Nan often likens the Ch'an Hall to the transforming fire of the ancient alchemists where sand is refined into gold, so intense and concentrated is our experience there.

Throughout the ages, Masters have each used their own methods, adapted to the time and talents and abilities of their particular disciples. Although the fundamental principles remain always and everywhere the same, it should be remembered that this lively Ch'an is also very personal. Master Nan's answers to a student's questions are often for *that* person in *that* state at *that* moment only, and not necessarily to be applied as blanket advice to anyone at any time. He answers questions in public, rather than individually in a private room in order that everyone may benefit from his answers, and to be sure that full understanding is openly reached and that everyone knows nothing false or incomplete has been given out as Truth.

Master Nan uses the *hua-t'ou* technique of meditation as the focus of this particular training. Each year the training is somewhat different, however, and many of these participants have been meditating for many years using a wide variety of methods and techniques from various traditions. The hua-t'ou is a paradoxical or even meaningless saying or phrase. The term itself literally means "thought's head," hence the occasional jokes about only being able to reach the thought's tail. It is a technique that anyone may use under the guidance of a qualified teacher with great benefit. It was developed by enlightened masters who taught their disciples to concentrate their attention on the mind, but not on the hua-t'ou itself, to concentrate the mind and realize the Self Nature.

Master Nan says we must *ts'an* the hua-t'ou. Ts'an means "ultimate participation in" or "complete penetration of" the hua-t'ou, of the mind. It is a word with such a depth of significance that we have not found any equivalent single word with its special impact in English, so we have retained this Chinese term throughout the book.

Another Chinese term which is found throughout the book is *ch'i*. In the *Yellow Emperor's Internal Medicine Classic*[2] it says that ch'i aids in blood circulation. Chinese herbal medicine principles claim that all illnesses first arise from a malfunction of ch'i circulation. Western medicine has used dissection to try to locate ch'i and ch'i routes, but to no avail since, after death, ch'i ceases. It is a vital force, a function, not a thing or an organ. Its so-called substance is of so subtle a nature as to be beyond the reach of our present technology.

Taoist and esoteric practices begin from the perfection of ch'i, thereby overcoming all the obstacles of the physical body. Their first result is excellent health. The second step in such cultivation is to reach samadhi. Confucian and Ch'an practitioners do not begin with cultivating ch'i, but on the contrary, they start from the cultivation of mind. The circulation of ch'i is automatically regulated by culti-

---

[2]From the Han Dynasty. For a complete list of references for the ancient Chinese texts referred to throughout this book, see the listing of Chinese Sources.

vating the mind, and thus improved health of the physical body naturally follows.

With regard to ch'i and other physical aspects of meditation referred to in this book, it is well not to dismiss these as superstition or vague oriental ideas, but to regard them rather in a scientific spirit and investigate further for oneself. More information about the physical aspects of meditation can be found in *Tao and Longevity: Mind-Body Transformation* by Master Nan, translated by Dr. Wen Kuan Chu.[3] We are encouraged to prove the truth of Ch'an teachings for ourselves, rather than to take anyone's word for it.

Readers should look over the Glossary at the back of this book, as it contains notes on people, places and terms that appear in the text and may not be familiar to general readers. Those conversant with Buddhist literature may notice discrepancies in dates or spellings from those they have read elsewhere. This is due to the fact that English sources often differ, and we have depended almost entirely on Chinese sources. Names of masters are also inconsistent among translations and so we have included the complete names in the Glossary, both personal and place names.

Frequently during the Master's monologues, he quotes – seemingly out of the blue – from another master or another source. These poems and quotes would have been familiar to the participants in the training session, but more importantly, they are bits and pieces the master meant to be heard and internalized – to enlighten and instruct. Because many Western readers may be unfamiliar with sayings from ancient Chinese texts, we have added some sources where necessary to clarify the Master's meaning. Some Chinese terms have been similarly explained in the text in brackets. It was important to us, in preparing this translation, to try to preserve the flow of what the Master was saying, so that you, the reader, could *participate* in the text, as though you, too, were there to hear it – without

---

[3]Wen Kuan Chu, *Tao and Longevity: Mind-Body Transformation,* published in 1984 by Samuel Weiser, Inc., York Beach, Maine.

constantly having to flip to the Glossary to understand the meaning.

We would like to stress again that this book is not intended as a scholarly work on Buddhism. Those who look for facts in this book will certainly find them, but it is not the facts which are of most importance here, but the sum of the experience. That which is within and above and behind fact and experience both is the aim of this book.

Prologue

Predawn darkness, piercing cold and full of the sound of the winter wind and rain in the trees outside. Water and wind sounds begin to give way to the softer sounds of people rousing from sleep. Some have already made their way in the darkness to the meditation hall. Some shuffle quietly about their early morning wake-up routines as others burrow under quilts for a few extra minutes of sleep.

We are savoring the warmth and comfort of our beds, and the quiet, knowing that by tonight bodily comfort will be gone, replaced by the aches and assorted pains that usually accompany the first days of an intensive effort by bodies unused to walking and sitting in meditation for prolonged periods. Since the first period does not begin until 5:30 – before breakfast! – we also have time to reflect on yesterday, our first day of Ch'an training.

We learned that our lives are to be reduced to essentials. We will eat, sleep and meditate. During the training, silence will alternate with speech, walking with sitting, just as rest and activity follow each other in our daily lives. The morning passed quickly as Master Nan explained what we would be doing, and why. He explained how to sit, walk and also about the "incense board." Never will he use this three-foot-long sword-like board to strike anyone! He told us of its origin and purpose:

During the Sung Dynasty, Master Ta Hui Kao was known to carry a split bamboo stick that served him as a walking stick, a pointer when teaching, and so on. Many monks, following the original rule of the Sangha from the Buddha's time also carried a walking stick surmounted by interlocking rings from which hung chains that rattled to announce their presence, and which they also used for effect when expounding. The walking stick may be a distant forerunner of the incense board; however, it was not until the Ch'ing Dynasty that the incense board, as we now know it, came into existence.

The Emperor Yung Cheng [1923-1835] was also an adept, and personally taught Ch'an methods to Buddhist and Taoist monks. Once there was a monk who had practiced for many years but could not reach enlightenment. Yung Cheng considered him to have potential, and so one day summoned him to report to the palace, where the monk was put in a room with a sword. He was told to do his own training for seven days, and if he could not reach enlightenment, he was to use the sword to kill himself. At the end of the seven days, he had still not succeeded and begged for another week, which was granted. At last, after the second seven days in seclusion, the monk succeeded.

From that day forward, a wooden sword, similar to the monk's sword, was used in many Ch'an Halls. This wooden sword was called an "incense board." Gradually, it was modified – becoming wider and less pointed. It came to be used to maintain order in the Ch'an Halls – proctors carried it in the meditation hall to remind meditators when they violated regulations. If someone fell asleep during meditation, for example, the proctor would use the board to lightly touch the sleeper, or if someone's posture was incorrect the board could be used to gently correct him. It was never used to hit or beat anyone in the meditation hall during Ch'an training. Master Nan has never personally known of anyone being enlightened or their karma being removed because of being hit by the board!

The Master went on to explain about our meals, sleeping arrangements, and so on, and told us our schedule: half-hour periods of sitting and walking meditation alternating throughout the day, beginning at 5:30 in the morning. We will stop for breakfast at 6:00 AM, and resume meditation at 7:30. After lunch at noon, we will rest until 2:00 PM, take a short break at 4:00 for a snack, and have dinner at 6:00 or so. The evening sessions will begin at 7:30, and end with a discussion period and a snack before bed.

Someone asked, "Why so many meals?" and Master Nan explained that we must all eat sparingly so we will not have trouble with our digestion or our ch'i during meditation. Since we will be working very hard, we must eat more often in small amounts, and we will eat a strictly vegetarian menu for all our meals.

During the first meditation period, we sat on our cushions. The Master sat before us, alert, sometimes silent and sometimes speaking. He discouraged note-taking. We must not use our ordinary minds to listen as we usually do, collecting information. We must attend with our *heart*, with our whole being, as a process of attention. The more we *don't* try to hold on to his actual words, the more fully will we experience their value, and arrive at the essential experience itself.

The walking meditation that followed the first period was a vigorous striding around the perimeter of the hall, swinging our arms. Master Nan paced the center of our circle, the incense board held upright behind his back. He didn't speak as we walked, except occasionally to encourage us to pick up our spirits and walk more energetically. Suddenly he hit the board full-length on the floor with a resounding smack, halting everyone in their tracks, knocking the last vestiges of idle thoughts completely out of our minds. We stood for a moment, and then he spoke to us for a while as we stood still, most of us with eyes closed.

And so each meditation followed, alternately walking or sitting. Sometimes we would walk and stop again, and he would talk for awhile; sometimes we would walk for a long time and return to our seats without a word being spoken.

During lunch we ate quietly – chatting was discouraged – and dinner passed likewise, mostly in silence. As we were dismissed to eat, or during our brief breaks following periods of walking meditation, people would approach the Master to ask private questions.

In the evening we resumed our sitting and walking meditation. Then came the discussion period – the Master said if we had no questions to ask him, he would question us! This continued for two hours or more until the Master dismissed us to get some sleep. Some of us sat in meditation for a while longer, but eventually the hall once again became empty, except for the silent presence of the Buddha.

Grass Mountain

A ch'an training week
held at
Chu Shih Lin
Hsin Pei-t'ou
Yang Ming Shan
Taiwan

Day One

10:15 AM: Second Day of the First Lunar Month

[Master Nan rings the gong three times, lights three sticks of incense and offers them before the Buddha. He begins to address the assembly:]

Our last Ch'an training week was two years ago. This year it was Mr. Yang, Mr. Hsiao, and Professor Chang who proposed the retreat, and now all the conditions have matured. Ancient masters said that Ch'an is like the water in the great sea: its supply fills every need.

During these seven days I will play the part of the Master. Afterwards we will be friends again. If any of you should reach enlightenment during these seven days, it will be your own enlightenment. It will not be because of anything I am doing to "enlighten" you.

The Ancients said that in order to expound and practice the Dharma, every single word must come from the deep field of Mind. Anything I say during this week should be considered and understood as coming direct from the Tao.

During these seven days I am the only one who is right. Whatever I may say is not to be taken as directed to any one specific individual. Absolutely do not look at it with your ordinary mind. If you neglect this instruction, all will be of no use.

All of you must throw away all of your previously acquired knowledge, principles, Taoist practices. Begin now from the beginning! If you can completely throw all that out, you will surely benefit. After the seven days we will all resume our former friendships if you like.

We will do sitting meditation for thirty minutes, followed by thirty minutes of walking meditation. You must not look around. Follow the group's schedule for all your daily needs – meals, sleeping, and so forth. Professor Chang must keep silence. The rest of you will not chat or do a lot of unnecessary talking. Those who do not know how to sit in meditation may ask Mr. Yang or Mr. Lu to teach you.

10:55 AM: First Period

Master: The Ch'an Sect has no standard teaching method, so it is called the "Gateless Gate." Ancient masters had no set way, so they invented an ingenious method: ts'an hua-t'ou. I will now give you three hua-t'ou and you can choose one. Those who have already made some progress in your Ch'an practice must also choose a hua-t'ou. Absolutely do not feel you are too smart! You must forget everything before this moment.

What is a hua-t'ou? That is a big question.

First of all, the hua-t'ou: the first one is "Who is repeating the Buddha's name?" or "Who is meditating?" The thought "repeating the Buddha's name " represents all of your thoughts.

The second hua-t'ou is "What was my original face before I was born?" This hua-t'ou also includes "Where was

I before I was born? Where will I go after death?" and "Where is *I*?"

The third hua-t'ou is "When there are no thoughts and no dreams, where is my true self?" or "Who is this bright, vivid self?" or "What is the source of my thoughts?" The first includes the latter two.

How do we ts'an hua-t'ou? Do not comment on it. Do not use a logical method. Do not expect enlightenment. Don't throw away the hua-t'ou looking for tranquility. Don't reason with yourself.

Disregard all your feelings – painful, peaceful – whatever they may be. The outside world has nothing to do with you. Cut it off! Continue to work in this manner.

Above all, you should do this strictly for yourselves. You must not do this to make me look good. If you have come here for my sake, that's a real joke! I'm not after fame or money.

Do not lower your head. Do not trifle with idle thoughts. Don't waste your time! When you hear me strike the wooden fish three times, begin to meditate. When the hand chime rings three times, we will begin walking meditation, striding vigorously around the perimeter of the Buddha Hall. When you hear the incense board drop, stop immediately.

If your legs are very painful, don't indulge them, but also don't force them: you must relax and not constrain them. Don't use force. Relax! You must very gently concentrate your mind into one. Pay no attention to all the feelings of your physical body.

11:30 AM: End First Period

Master: Walking, standing, sitting, reclining: every moment you must let go of everything and take care of your hua-t'ou. A lot of you are not yet on the track with the hua-t'ou. Too many idle thoughts. You yourselves haven't yet really made a firm resolution. This is all up to you – you cannot depend on other people.

The meaning of a hua-t'ou for Ch'an people is summed up in just one word: *doubt*. The ancients said: "Great doubt: great enlightenment; Small doubt: small enlightenment; No doubt, no enlightenment."

"Who am I?" "I am who?" – I don't want you to think yourselves around in circles, but just keep chasing after that question, "Who am I?" Don't let your mind wander. The best time to look into a hua-t'ou is when your mind is not drowsy or wandering. We call just a little wayward mind "restlessness." Hold your mind gently in oneness. Stay with your hua-t'ou.

1:15 PM: After Lunch Break

Master: Half a day is already gone. This retreat is an opportunity that we don't easily get, so work diligently on your hua-t'ou. Just as in cooking only *you* can control the time and temperature. Your mind must do nothing except hold this hua-t'ou.

Tao is already there. It is formless, directionless, positionless, not wandering, not drowsy. It is pure and bright just as it is. This is Right Mind. It is not easy to attain this state.

Beginners in Ch'an must concentrate their minds into one as a first step. Beat the idle thoughts completely to death and there is Right Mind. Simply hold your mind in oneness – disregard enlightenment or no enlightenment! Expecting enlightenment is just another idle thought. The Neo-Confucianists considered idle thoughts as guests who come and go; they are not the master of the house.

Don't get drowsy! Pick yourself up! Work on your mind *with* your mind. Don't get lazy with the hua-t'ou. Those of you who have already made some progress must also concentrate on your hua-t'ou.

Since the Ch'ing Dynasty, most practitioners in the Ch'an halls have been taught to look into a hua-t'ou, but very few of them have accomplished anything. On the contrary, I witnessed that many people in the Ch'an halls would ts'an hua-t'ou to the extreme that they vomited blood. It will do you no good to kill yourself meditating. Therefore, to be too intense about the hua-t'ou is also no use. If you can concentrate your mind, then someday there will come a day of deliverance as a matter of course.

There are a couple of you who are already on the track. All of you must be so diligent that "Mount T'ai could collapse in front of you and you would not be moved. A magical deer could appear beside you but you would not even blink your eyes."[4] This means you must stop your mind.

If you are right on the track, when you walk you are not aware of walking; looking, you are not aware of looking. Everything in the outside world has nothing to do with you. If you can work assiduously enough to reach this state, then you can make progress. Go back to your seats and look well into your hua-t'ou!

1:22 PM: Second Period

Master: Taoists and Buddhists say that drowsiness is a demon; sleep is also a demon. [*During walking meditation:*] The first period is already past, and most of you have spent it half drowsy. Gold will never shine without the refining fire! Swing your arms wide! Chest up! Lift up your spirits! Hold your mind gently in one. Guard your hua-t'ou!

---

[4]From the *Analects,* the sayings of Confucius compiled by Tseng Tze.

Don't be indulgent. Once you lose your attention you can make no progress.

One person among us is a "Causal Ground Bodhisattva." This one has already been practicing Buddhism for several decades. He is able to see many states of mind. He decided to come over here to ts'an ch'an. He plans to throw away all his previous practices in order to start all over again.

A hua-t'ou means "Stop!" All idle thoughts are beaten to death. A hua-t'ou means contemplating "Who is repeating Buddha's name?" A hua-t'ou is a method like reciting Buddha's name to concentrate the mind.

Great heroes and men of noble spirit have the ability to concentrate their minds. Great evil men also have this power. When concentration is great enough, even gold and stone can be cracked open. The power of a hua-t'ou has great force. It is not the power of the hua-t'ou itself, however, but the power of the mind. After your spirit is concentrated, you will also automatically be in control of your ch'i.

I am not kidding! You young people pay attention! Take care of your hua-t'ou, don't play with your idle thoughts.

Ts'an hua-t'ou is not the same as reciting the Buddha's name. Reciting Buddha's name must be continuous – you don't stop – with great faith. While you ts'an hua-t'ou, however, you must have doubt. You must chase it within yourself. Ts'an includes studying it, suspecting it, and so on. Diligently ts'an hua-t'ou! Go back to your seats.

2:30 PM: Third period

Master: [*He strikes the wooden fish three times.*] Why do Buddhists use the wooden fish? It is said that fish never close their eyes, day and night. Buddhist training wants us to learn from the way of the fish: never resting, never sleeping. We must get rid of sleepiness in order to practice zealously. If you feel sleepy, take a deep breath, hold it for a while and open your eyes.

3:05 PM: Walking

Master: Can ts'an hua-t'ou be used like a mantra? If your mind is not sincere, not truly concentrated, no mantra will work. If your mind is sincere, ts'an hua-t'ou will have the same effect as a mantra.

You have all been in a half drowsy state. Now everyone is no longer drowsy, but you are full of idle thoughts instead. I would rather hope that you would all go back to that half drowsy state again. Control your own eyes, so you can gradually gather your mind back to the center again. Hold your mind! Hold your heads up!

3:25 PM: Fourth Period

Master: Time passes like lightning, so you must work very hard. If your legs can't stand it, you can loosen them up, but you must not loosen up your inner mind. Hold your hua-t'ou! If your legs can stand it, you had better be patient.

To simply hold your hua-t'ou does not mean to hold down other thoughts. Just hold your hua-t'ou and your idle thoughts will automatically disappear.

Some of you people who have already gotten into it a little must also hold the hua-t'ou. It's just like someone walking with a walking stick. Even though the stick can't do the walking for you, you feel better if you have one in your hand.

3:55 PM: Ten Minutes Rest

Master: Hold your hua-t'ou – don't relax! Take care of that hua-t'ou, don't indulge yourself.

There are several possible sidetracks when looking into a hua-t'ou. Some people look into the hua-t'ou but at the same time they play with their idle thoughts. That doesn't get you anywhere. Even if you seem to gain something, it is only an empty blossom, or the moon in the river. You cannot accomplish anything.

Some people are in a state as if they were dwelling in a dark, icy cave full of ghosts. Still others feel their ch'i moving and feel as if they had reached Tao. All of these things should be disregarded! They only arise because the hua-t'ou is not being used most effectively.

You must concentrate with one mind. You must not reason with yourself. All of those are erroneous mind. Your knowledge or scholarship actually has no roots. You really don't know. Therefore you should never make comments. Any reason you can express with your mouth is nothing but "lip-service-Ch'an."

Ou-Yang Ching-wu was a great teacher of Buddhism. When he was dying he said to his disciples: "All I have learned in my life is of no use in this moment. I advise you to stay on the main path, sincerely reciting Buddha's name."

At this time each of you must individually work hard. It is not easy to find such an opportunity. Time passes by very easily, so we must get something out of it.

4:30 PM: Fifth Period

Master: First you must start from inside your mind. It is said that inner sincerity reflects outward. Next, your outward posture must be correct. First comes discipline; only then can samadhi and wisdom be developed.

Mr. Chang! Stop frowning! Try to wear a smile on your face.

5:05 PM: End Meditation Period

Master: In the *Ch'an Men Jih Sung* it says: "The day has passed and life is shortened. We are like fish in evaporating water; what happiness can there be?" If you are truly diligent, there will always be a reward. Your efforts will never be wasted. The most difficult thing for human beings to manage is themselves. Mr. Wang Yang-ming said: "It is easy to get rid of bandits in the mountains, but difficult to get rid of the bandits in one's mind." It is especially difficult to control one's own mind.

Some people ask why Sakyamuni picked up the flower, and why Kasyapa smiled. Why indeed? Ts'an diligently! Today is almost gone. It is up to you to find the answer to this question.

5:30 PM: Sixth Period

Master: During this period, some of you are doing pretty well. Only your legs are giving you a little trouble.

Master Huang Lung Nan gave this example concerning ts'an hua-t'ou: It should be like "a very clever cat trying to catch a rat: a steady eye without a blink, four feet firmly on the mark, all senses focused straight ahead, head and tail straight."

Where do you come from at birth? Where do you go at death? Do not try to guess! You must prove it. If you can see through the hua-t'ou, then you can solve this riddle. This is the so-called "p'o-ts'an," the first stage in Ch'an training.

In the universe, the highest truth is absolutely ordinary. Ordinary people, however, have no wisdom, and are always looking for something mysterious instead. A practitioner must find this treasure, which is not worth a single penny. After enlightenment, you can truly understand that the highest is the most ordinary.

Hold your hua-t'ou! Don't relax! Today it's not cold, not hot; a really fine day. Just right for working hard.

7:10 PM:

Master: Working on our hua-t'ou, as we have been today, we can't get anywhere. What we must do is to make ourselves like living dead. We are not considered on the track until we reach this state.

If you want to drop your worldly affairs, you must drop them unconditionally. For example, since we are here, we have dropped everything down the mountain behind us, haven't we?

If our understanding is complete but our practice is not, then understanding is futile. If our practice is complete but our understanding is not, practice is useless also. In the old days, people who sought Tao often neglected their lives. Several decades from now, people will call *us* the "people of the old days." We must set an example for the next generation, so later people can learn from us.

7:30-8:00 PM: Seventh Period

Master: Whether the rules are strict or lenient during this retreat, both are right.

Who is it that is able to think? You must bring all of your mind together into one mind. Pursue that hua-t'ou all the way to the very end! Don't just work on your body.

8:25-9:00 PM:

Sitting meditation.

9:00 PM: Discussion Period

Master: According to our schedule we should meditate until 11:30, but this evening we will loosen up a little. Tomorrow we will get up at 6:00 and begin meditation at 6:30. Every evening we will have a discussion. If you have any questions, you can ask them at that time. If you have no questions, I will question you.

Upasaka Huang: In the past, the way I ts'an hua-t'ou was just to comment. If the way to ts'an hua-t'ou is to control the mind in one place, and empty both body and mind, I want to know whether or not it is the same as continuously purifying the mind by repeating Buddha's name. Master please instruct me.

Master: Ts'an hua-t'ou is *not* controlling the mind in one place and it is *not* for the purpose of emptying body and mind. Nevertheless, what is the purpose of ts'an hua-t'ou? You ts'an for yourself!

Mr. Hsia: In the afternoon my legs were painful, so I had even more idle thoughts.

Mr. Lin: My idle thoughts rose again and again, and I couldn't limit them.

Mr. Chu: I was very sleepy today. I was drowsy all the time.

Mr. Ch'eng: Whatever the Master tells me to do, I do.

Mr. Chang: For the past year I have been close to the Master, but I didn't spend much time on Buddhism. I have been studying logic. Therefore, while looking into the hua-t'ou I kept on using a logical method on it. I feel like killing myself, and I want to throw out a grenade too. In the future, I may be very much against Buddhism and all of the traditional disciplines. It may be possible that I'll go to hell.

Upasaka Lu: I wish our afternoon nap could be longer, to avoid feeling drowsy during meditation.

Upasaka Liu: When I participated in a Ch'an retreat before, everything was all mixed up. Today my ts'an hua-t'ou didn't really get on the track. I could feel ch'i moving through my body and at the same time, I could still hold my hua-t'ou.

Upasika Liu: All day today I have been confused and drowsy.

Mr. Sun: When I ts'an hua-t'ou by using the concept of doubt, the more I do it, the more bored I feel. I feel that ts'an hua-t'ou is itself attached to something, therefore I only used insight and heaven and earth became One. The hua-t'ou was also not forgotten.

Professor Chang: I was fine from four to five in the afternoon. Before that I was drowsy all the time. When I meditate at home, I can calm down after ten or fifteen minutes, but when I ts'an "Who is repeating Buddha's name?" I cannot relax. On the contrary, I felt very tense.

Mrs. Fu: During the afternoon, I looked into "Who is repeating Buddha's name?" but it wasn't as good as last year. I couldn't meditate, either.

Miss T'ang: While looking into the hua-t'ou, I always want to find an explanation and I also feel like crying. I was only on the track for a very short period of time.

Mrs. Chou: I used "Who is repeating Buddha's name?"

Mrs. Yang: I made up my mind to work hard and I also resolved to ts'an to the best of my ability.

Mr. Hsiao: The Master's teaching today was really inspiring to me.

Upasaka Fu: During the first period, when I used "When there are no thoughts and no dreams, where is my true self?" I only made comments. During the second period, I thought that to ts'an hua-t'ou is to control the mind in one place. After four o'clock it got better. The last two periods I dropped it, and stopped ts'an hua-t'ou altogether. I feel even better and very clear.

Mr. Ch'in: I'm frightened, because I have read very few sutras and haven't done much practicing. In the afternoon at four o'clock, I experienced a very fine state and felt very comfortable. The ch'i in my ears has started to circulate.

Mr. Yang: Today is the first time I ever ts'an hua-t'ou. I feel meditation is only a part of cultivation. In the afternoon I used "Who is repeating Buddha's name?" More or less on the track, I made up my mind to get somewhere.

Professor Hsieh: I used "Who is meditating?" When my thoughts disappeared, I didn't ts'an anymore.

Mr. Lio: All I can do is ts'an the tail of the hua-t'ou. I couldn't ts'an the hua-t'ou. I hope someday the bottom of the barrel drops out!

Mr. Hsiang: In the past I used to have a lot of idle thoughts. Today, while looking into the hua-t'ou, my idle thoughts were much fewer.

Master: First, some people doubt the hua-t'ou. Second, some people have dropped their hua-t'ou and ceased to ts'an. Third, some people were only fooling around with their own methods.

All of these can be excused with the single exception of Mr. Chang, who is not right. He has refused to throw away his previous learning, and refused to let his mind calm down.

Today our record is not too bad. Whether you can or cannot hold your hua-t'ou is all up to you, but I hope you are willing to let me hook you for seven days. Listen to me, obey me for seven days.

You must listen to everything I say. My word is poison, and you shouldn't listen, but if you don't listen to me your illness cannot be cured. Attainment is attainment, it is not Tao. You must keep this in mind!

Day Two

第二天

6:11 AM: Walking Meditation

Master: When you first wake up – before you have moved a hand or foot – is a good time to practice. Lao-tze used the word "meek," and Mencius the phrase "the restorative influence of the night" to say that the mind is very clear in that state. If we keep the mind clear and bright like "the calm air of morning," that's excellent.

Mr. Chang, lift up your head! Shoulders back! Even though you are fooling around with your idle thoughts, you're doing better that way.

When you first wake up, you must ts'an "How did I wake up?" People who are diligent will all pay attention to each of these moments. The ancients used ascetic practices. Modern practitioners do the same.

Yesterday we used the ts'an hua-t'ou method. This has been used since the late Sung or early Yuan period. Its founder was Master Kao Feng. At the present time, people accept mere lip-service-Ch'an as Ch'an Buddhism.

During and before the Sung, there were hua-t'ou but they didn't ts'an. When asked, "What is Buddha?" there would be an answer: "Mind is Buddha." The next question is, "What is Mind?" The answer is "Not Mind, not Buddha."

Usually, hua-t'ou are of two kinds. One is questions and answers, like: "Who is repeating Buddha's name?" and so forth. The second kind is meaningless, like: "Dry shit," or "Spruce tree in the front yard."

The Ch'an Sect seeks liberation by wisdom, but since the very beginning not a single person has been enlightened without samadhi. The old masters said, "Those who can't reach enlightenment should go do some practicing."

How does one practice? The answer is *discipline*; practice samadhi, gain wisdom. Yan Yang asked: "If I have nothing with me, then what?" Master Chao-chou answered him by loudly shouting "You drop it!" Yan Yang then asked: "If I have nothing with me, how can I drop it?" Chao-chou answered: "If you cannot drop it, carry it along with you." This way of teaching [as a dialogue] was used before the Yuan Dynasty. [*A pause*] Early in the morning, your ch'i should be completely without disturbance. According to Mencius' way of nourishing our nighttime ch'i, if you work on this over a long period of time, you can cultivate the mind so that it fills up the universe.

"A great man has a will of his own, like a rocket shooting to heaven, not following even the Tathagata's way." A truly great man must act this way. In the old days some people reached enlightenment within wealthy and honored circles, and some were even enlightened while mingling with entertainers. None of them took the same route as Sakyamuni.

"Mind is Buddha." What is Mind? First, there is the mind of idle thoughts. Second, there is the universal mind.

> Not the movement of the wind.
> Not the movement of the flag.
> It is the movement of the Mind.
>   [*Platform Sutra* of the Sixth Patriarch]

If you think your idle thoughts mind is Ch'an, that is a great mistake.

"There is a prostitute among us, but in mind there is no prostitute." If you have more experience in practicing, you can reach this level of non-discrimination. There is nothing strange about it. It's nothing great, either. The *Surangama Sutra* says: "Mountains, rivers [the physical world of manifestation] all appear from the wondrous, bright True Mind."

Is the Mind moved? Where is the Mind? Ts'an! Drop everything. Let go of everything connected with the outside world! This is IT right here! When you lose your temper, is that IT? Why isn't it clear and pure, then? The monk Pao-chih said:

> The great Tao is always before you,
> And yet it is very hard to see.

There is nothing! Drop everything! Go back to your seats.

6:45-7:20 AM: First Period

Master: Drop everything! Don't concentrate on keeping the One, either. If you have a feeling of being clear and bright, it is already long gone.

7:40 AM: Walking

Master: Don't think idle thoughts! Drop them! Drop them — that's it. Hmm! If you have "drop it" in your mind that's already another mistake. [*Master Nan hits the incense board loudly and asks:*] What is *it*? Recognize this clearly! People don't recognize the Tao that is right in front of their eyes. Clever people play around with their idle thoughts all day long. Dull people don't recognize this.

Around the time of Sung, ancient masters used the "Gateless Dharma Gate" to help people get rid of all entanglements. People who practice enthusiastically get entangled in their practice – you must not be attached to any method or practice.

Ch'an Master Huang P'o said: "During the great T'ang Dynasty there are no Ch'an masters. I don't mean there is no Ch'an, I only mean there are no Ch'an masters." Ch'an is eternal. There are sages in the East and sages in the West. Their Mind is the same. Their principles are the same.

Drop everything! Drop the "drop it"! If after you let go of everything, there is a clear and bright feeling there, it proves you have already become attached to something. Experience this exact moment! Experience this very moment! Realize this very moment more and more.

Why has the Ch'an Sect gotten weaker? Up through the T'ang Dynasty, the country was very strong. Ch'an masters were all great heroes and men of great courage. Since the late Sung, however, Ch'an became the Ch'an of virtuous men.[5] What can we say about the Ch'an Sect now? The *Diamond Sutra* says:

> It is beyond all forms and is
> identical with all things (Dharmas).

The First Patriarch said:

> All outer causes cease;
> No huff and puff in the mind.
> Mind like a wall
> Tao can then be sought.

---

[5]It seems necessary to further understand what is meant by the term "virtuous men." Virtuous men are very good, but in their goodness they are also lacking the nerve to do great things. Originally, Ch'an was intended only for those who were of great courage and who had broad minds. For example, a killer might drop his knife and become immediately enlightened by the act. Good or bad as a virtue is not the issue here. Enlightenment depends on the capacity of the mind. *Tr.*

This is only the way of cultivation. He didn't have people ts'an hua-t'ou, but the hua-t'ou method is already in this teaching.

How do we talk about Ch'an? [*Master Nan pauses for a brief silence, then continues:*] That's it. You haven't listened. I haven't said anything.

8:15-8:45 AM: Second Period

Silent meditation.

8:45 AM:

Master: In the last part of the later Han, Buddhism was introduced from India into China. Fu Tu Ch'eng used his superphysical powers during the time to promote Buddhism. Superphysical powers develop out of samadhi. Chih-kuan and Dhyana are all related to samadhi.

Later, Kumarajiva came to China and translated many of the Sutras. Dharma Master Hui Yuan founded the Pure Land Sect, whose practice is the repeating of Buddha's name in order to be reborn in the Western Paradise. This method is very safe, and proceeds from emptiness to fullness. Later, the First Patriarch came to China. He taught Emptiness: from emptiness to extreme emptiness. As years passed, people's innate spiritual potential was not as high, so the Ch'an Sect developed methods like the hua-t'ou to help them, but this method also gave people an attachment.[6]

---

[6]This is a typical buddhist idea: that in earlier times, people had greater ability, which diminishes over time from the original idea or teacher; therefore we need methods to help us. Parts of the *Lotus Sutra* speak of the "diminishing age" of the dharma when few will hear, and fewer will understand. *Tr.*

How do we ts'an? We must do it apart from consciousness. Ts'an! "Tranquility," "Transcendence." Those are only your consciousness. You should not mistake it for your original self. You must discover that which *makes* you tranquil, *makes* you transcendent. My words are poison, but if you don't listen, your sickness cannot be cured.

"Drop it" is just "drop it." Even your "drop it" must be dropped. Just like that! Drop it!

Everything in the physical universe is just as it is. If you study or seek Tao, you must have an extra eye [i.e., wisdom]. When your Tao is one foot high, the obstacles will be ten feet high. If you resolve to cultivate yourself, obstacles arise. Don't play with idle thoughts. Do not be afraid. It is "what ten eyes behold; what ten fingers point at."

Everyone who is on this mountain for seven days must be grateful to all living beings who have contributed directly or indirectly to this special opportunity. People shouldn't "murmur against Heaven, nor grumble against men"; even if you are doomed to starve to death, you might as well accept it with a comfortable and peaceful mind.

9:30-10:00 AM: Third Period

Master: Tidy up your body and mind. Don't focus your mind at a certain place inside your body. You must also not focus on emptiness or the void. How can we *not* concentrate or focus? Let your mind out the top of your head, leaving behind this bunch of bones sitting here. Remember: don't cling to form!

Ch'an Sect doctrine is prajna. Prajna is an essential doctrine of Buddhism, and is True Reality. The essence of prajna is when one can practically empty the body and mind, becoming united with the universe. A state of prajna and a state of "light" are associated with the state of

"Ch'ing-an" – a very light, peaceful state of concentration; an early stage of samadhi. Liberation by prajna is the experience of "no wisdom and no gain." [*Heart Sutra*]

What are the three seals of Dharma-truth? They are Emptiness [no-mind], No Form, and No-intention [no clinging]. Attainment [that is, practice] is not prajna. Attainment can be achieved through cultivation, but will someday certainly be destroyed. Prajna is eternal, and is not created and not destroyed.

Ch'an Master Huai Jang guided Ma Tzu saying: "If I can't make a mirror by polishing a brick, how can you make a Buddha by meditation?" How then can we make ourselves into Buddhas?

The *Doctrine of the Mean* says: "The hawk flies up to heaven; The fishes leap in the deep."

> The sea is wide enough
> for fish to jump,
> The sky is broad enough
> for birds to fly . . .

So let your wandering thoughts alone. Why use force to control them? But still, you must get rid of them. A grain of dust in your eye can blind you. A diamond particle in your eye will also blind you. Knowledge, wealth and honor, attaining Tao, attaining great skill in practice – all of these can make us fall into the trap of pride. It is not easy to get rid of these things.

Ch'an Master Ma Tzu tweaked Pai Chang's nose. When it really hurt, Pai Chang was enlightened. What was Pai Chang's enlightenment? Don't play with your idle thoughts. Just ts'an!

10:30-11:00 AM: Fourth Period

Silent meditation.

11:00 AM: Walking

Master: Ma Tzu looked at a duster and Pai Chang said: "It is the use. It is apart from the use." Ma Tzu asked him: "In the future when you flap your lips, what kind of a teacher will you be?" Pai Chang took the duster and held it up, and Ma Tzu then said: "It is the use. It is apart from the use."

After everything has been let go, then function itself can arise. Pai Chang then took the duster and hung it back where it had been, and Ma Tzu then gave a great shout. The shout made Pai Chang deaf for three days. Was he truly deaf? Actually, for those three days his idle thoughts were absolutely stopped.

Let it go, let it go. Let the mind be very clean. Pay no attention to anything. Now, don't play with your idle thoughts. Walk!

If you study Ch'an, your understanding must surpass the teacher's. Don't let me fool you! Pai Chang said:

> The lively brilliance shines alone,
> Having completely shaken off
> the senses and their qualities.
> The essence reveals eternal Truth.
> Words and writing don't matter.
> Self-nature is without stain;
> Originally complete and perfect.
> Separate from confusion of causation
> Like the immutability of the Buddha.

Separate from the confusion of causation; immutability and immovability. That's it, but you are all still looking around for something else. Do you really want to look for something? Ok, there is a way: meditate, go look for it!

11:25-11:50 AM: Fifth Period

Master: After you fully understand this, you must also know how to harmonize it. How is it done when in motion and in stillness? You must harmonize it in your daily activities.

People ask: "What is the strange and special thing?" Pai Chang said: "Sitting all alone on the Buddha Peak." A monk heard this and bowed to him. Pai Chang hit the monk. It is no good for a man to be extremely outstanding but unable to be ordinary. That is only the level of the Small Vehicle.

Ancient masters didn't follow the beaten track. They seemed to have hands and eyes all over – they were ever observant and able to guide people. The Monk Mei Tzu said: "Let him [Ma Tzu] say 'no mind, no Buddha'; to me Mind is Buddha." Ma Tzu heard and said: "The plum is ripe."

Upasaka Pang asked Ma Tzu: "Who is the one who has nothing to do with all the Dharmas?" Ma Tzu answered: "I will tell you when you drink up all the water in the West River in one gulp." Upasaka Pang was thereupon enlightened. Then he sighed: "Difficult, so difficult, like spreading ten buckets of sesame oil on a tree!" Mrs. Pang answered: "Easy, so easy! The old masters' meaning is on the tips of the grasses." Their daughter Ling Chao said: "It is not difficult, not easy. When hungry, eat. When tired, sleep."

You are all studying Ch'an. Do you think it is difficult or easy? To die sitting down or standing up! One can master one's own death; the ancients could do it, but can you?

A great nun once said:

All day seeking spring
Unable to find it;
My straw sandals
Trample mountaintop clouds.
When I return, my hands reach out,
Full of plum blossoms' fragrance!
Spring is already complete
On the tips of the branches!

Where is it? It's right here! On your legs? [*Everyone laughs.*]

1:25 PM: Walking

Master: [*Hits the board.*] The sound of the board contains all sound and form, but people like to search in mysterious and abstruse places instead. If you can be sure, then you can really be absolutely complete. If you cannot be certain, then you are not complete.

Su Tung-po said: "The sound of the stream speaks into the whole universe. The form of the mountains is nothing but the form of Pure Dharma." The Buddha was so good at expounding the dharma that his tongue covered the entire universe. There was a Ch'an master who argued with Su Tung-po, saying: "If the stream is sound and the mountain is the form of dharma, how miserable things would be without them!"

In the *Analects* it says: "Do you think I am concealing something from you? I have nothing to hide from you." Master Mei T'ang asked Huang Shan-ku, "Can you smell the mu-hsi blossoms?" Huang said yes. Mei T'ang then said: "I have nothing to hide." Huang then had a realization.

Later Ch'an Master Sse Hsin Hsin asked Huang Shan-ku: "If a monk dies and scholar Huang dies, and they are cremated into two piles of ash, where do they meet each other?" Huang couldn't answer him.

If they *do* want to meet each other?...Drop it; then they can meet. Pick it up; then you can also get some idea.

Mr Yang: [*interrupting*] Seeing is not the essence of seeing.

Upasaka Lio: [*to Mr. Yang*] There isn't any such thing as "seeing is not the essence of seeing" in the cycle of birth and death.

Master: Huang Shan-ku had been demoted to a post in Chien-nan in northern Kiangsi Province. On his way there, he once stopped to nap during the day. And when he awoke, he suddenly reached enlightenment. What did he realize? Mr. Yang and Mr. Lio's comments just now are only lip-service Ch'an.

The *Avatamsaka Sutra* says: "The whole teaching of the *Avatamasaka Sutra* asserts that faith is the gate to

Buddahood." That is, not faith in other people, but belief in oneself. If you are sure of yourself, then you have come home. Those two Upasakas just expressed their feelings. Now I add mine: This matter is just like the "taste of salt in water, the glue in paint."[7] See if you can find out. Return to your seats.

Pay attention! Ts'an! Drop it. Care for nothing.

Mr. Yang: [*to himself*] It may be better if I don't see it.

Master: You must see it!

1:55-2:27 PM: Sixth period

Master: In the *Surangama Sutra* it says: "Even if you . . . preserve inner quiet, the shadow of [your] differentiation of things [dharma] still remains." Let go of it! Drop the physical shell, inside and out. "Trample on top of the essential body of Buddha-truth." [Break down even the Buddha Truth.] Don't care about your body; just see what it turns out to be. Don't be drowsy now. Sit up straight. [*Master Nan points to someone.*] You are too drowsy. Open your eyes a little. Right at this moment, drowsy or not, clear or not—where is your pure nature now?

Just as the salt in water is everywhere throughout the water, if you raise the temperature and remove the salt, the water is all pure again. An ancient master said:

> Wild goats hang by their horns in trees at night;
> No trace of them can be found on the ground.
> The East wind, too,
> Full of the Great Emptiness.

Do you understand?

---

[7]From a gatha by Fu Ta Shih.

3:00-3:30 PM: Seventh period

Master: [*as people are being seated*] When you've just got your legs arranged; that's IT. Right at that moment. After that your mind starts expecting samadhi, and it is again not IT. You must recognize the IT of this moment, but it isn't Tao. Ts'an! [*A period of silent meditation passes.*]

Master: During this period, all of you have been drowsy because you ate too much lunch. Your ch'i routes are all blocked up.

4:00 PM: Walking

Master: [*Hits the incense board.*]

> The false nature spontaneously rests.
> When it rests, there is exactly Bodhi.
> > [*Surangama Sutra*]

Drop it. After you drop it, that's IT. In the *Surangama Sutra* it tells that once there was a man in India who got up one morning and looked into the mirror. He thought the head in the mirror was very handsome, but he couldn't see his own head, so he went mad and looked all around everywhere for his head. Later, when he found his head, he was no longer mad.

When the Buddha was first enlightened, he said: "How strange! All living beings possess Tathagata Wisdom and Original Purity, but because they cling to their false thoughts they cannot witness it." When he witnessed his enlightenment, he wanted to enter Nirvana, but the Heavenly Being [Indra] knelt down before him and begged him to remain in the world. The Buddha replied: "Stop, stop! My Dharma is so marvellous it cannot be apprehended by thought."

Do you want to see your original face? Who has seen it? Human beings are the most pitiful creatures in the world, who cannot even perceive their own original nature. Would you like to see it? Let go of your idle thoughts. "The false nature spontaneously rests. When it rests, there is exactly Bodhi."

Lao Tze said: "We have great trouble because we have a body." He also said: "Disregard the self, and the self simply exists."

What should we do? First, you must forget self for others. Second, as far as your practice is concerned, you must fill up the universe – become one with heaven and earth. The dharma body perfectly pervades all the universe. How can we do it? We must drop it. Relax! Completely, totally rest your mind and let go of everything.

Actually, you have already reached this level, but you are only tied up by awareness of cultivation, and you are still seeking something strange and abstruse. Drop everything! Then you can perceive your original face. Don't let other people lead you by the nose. Ts'an!

Before the later Sung, Ch'an was just like this: very ordinary, very plain, but also very powerful. It was like a knife that can kill someone, but also like a sword that can save your life. Master Wu Tzu's method had a spirit like this: "Drive away the farmer's cow. Snatch the food away from a starving man."

Ch'an Master Lin Chi said: "Sometimes man is deprived, circumstances are not deprived" [ordinary people like to be flattered]; "Sometimes circumstances are deprived, and man is not deprived" [circumstances are not right]; "Sometimes both man and circumstances are deprived" [ignore them]; and "Sometimes neither man nor circumstances are deprived [let them go]."

There is no standard method by which to conveniently guide people. Rather, the method resembles a pearl rolling around in a dish: a living method that leads us to reach the state of "False nature spontaneously rests." Those who have truly achieved Tao are absolutely free of the limitations of birth and death.

4:34-5:04 PM: Eighth Period

Silent meditation.

5:04 PM: Walking

Master: [*hits the board*] Let it go! "False nature spontaneously rests; when it rests, there is exactly Bodhi." The *Diamond Sutra* says: "Past mind cannot be found, present mind cannot be found, future mind cannot be found.... Their minds should abide nowhere. Abiding nowhere, mind is developed" And also: "No form of a person, a self, a being or a life."

What is being? It is society. People, self, and society are all related in space. A life is related to time. The main principle of the *Diamond Sutra* is to empty out the four forms, and to get rid of the three minds [past, present, and future]. How can it be done? Cut off the three limitations. The three minds cannot be found. Don't try to hold onto them, but also don't try to get rid of them. Ancient masters said: "The top of the mountain of the five aggregates is the void. They use the same door passing in and out, yet never meet." You must stay aware of this emptiness.

People who have some power of samadhi are always very clear-minded, never drowsy or confused. [That is false emptiness.] Between past mind and future mind there is a block of emptiness. We must recognize this block of emptiness. [*The Master hits the board and says:*] Past mind cannot be found. Go back to your seats!

5:30-6:00 PM: Ninth Period

Master: Cut off the three limitations. Right after that moment is IT. However, you aren't able to maintain that state. Why is that? Understand why you must abide in the state of "Cut off the three limitations." At the moment when your mind initiates the movement of a thought, your mind should be clear and bright like a mirror. Gradually, gradually you will naturally abide in that state. It is very lively! Taoists call it "nourishing," and Buddhists call it "cultivating" this state.

After you see your nature, you then must begin cultivation. The Fifth Patriarch said: "Before you see your original nature, you can get no benefit from cultivation." Confucius said: "At fifteen I had my mind set on learning. At thirty I stood firm. At fourty, I had no doubts. At fifty, I knew the decrees of Heaven. At sixty, my ear was obedient [the mind was detached]. At seventy, I could follow what my heart desired, without transgressing what was right [always in samadhi]."

In Mencius' "Chin Hsin Chang" chapter, he discusses "nourishing ch'i." "Virtue is something that is welcomed by all [the joy of dhyana]." "The real is that which possesses perfect goodness [functioning always from the void, clear and bright]." "That which is full of goodness is called beauty [ch'i routes and spiritual essence complete]." "That which brightly displays its complete goodness is called Great." [This stage is beyond ordinary human understanding, equal to a Buddha's state.]

The *Surangama Sutra* says: "Reason can be suddenly enlightened, but daily matters [karma] cannot be suddenly removed." Take your time. Abide there. Don't hurry. Don't be too anxious. This shows us why in the old days, when people realized Tao, they would not leave their masters until after ten or twenty years, in order to learn more in detail.

The monk Tao Chi composed this poem:

> Both banks of the river:
>   peach blossoms red and fresh;
> Both sides of the dike:
>   willows' green green light.
> Far off, the egrets
>   at their fishing place
> Break the calm lake's
>   stillness.

In May the West Lake
   still cool as autumn,
And the floating scent
   of the lotus secret stirring.
Next year when blossoms fall
   where will I be?
I take up the wine
   and ask the nodding blooms.

Carefully nourish Tao. Don't cling to knowledge. Then every marvellous thought, all wonderful words will flow from your mouth [like Tao Chi].

7:00 PM: Walking

Master: [*hits the incense board*] Today I have been talking like Ch'an people did back in the Golden Age of the T'ang Dynasty: it is also ts'an.

I wonder if anyone here has attained the state of "three limitations cut off," and is dwelling in the state of natural stability. If you reach this state, it is called the realization of Tao. At the time of realization of Tao, you actually realize nothing. To realize Tao is relatively easy, but to cultivate Tao is very difficult. An ancient master once said: "Those who realize Tao through a sudden circumstance will never lose it."

If what you have realized is not true, however, and if what you have understood is incomplete, then what you must do is go to a very noisy, worldly place or a very rich and honored environment to refine yourself for cultivation. The greatest people retire into the highest echelons of government service. Lesser people retire into the ordinary world. Solitary men retire into mountains and forests.

In the wealthy and honored and sophisticated places, the busy and worldly places, obstacles to practice are everywhere. If you can unperturbedly dwell in samadhi, other people will never know that you have attained Tao. Yo Shan said it is like: "Standing on the summit of a lone mountain; Walking the deepest depths of the sea." As to how we refine ourselves in cultivation . . . I will talk about that tomorrow. Walk!

[After a while, he hits the board and continues:]

To be a teacher is the unluckiest thing under the sun! Ch'an Master Pai Chang once met an old wild fox in the form of an old man who said to him: "Someone asked me if a man of great cultivation was still subject to the law of causality. I replied: 'He is not subject to the law of causality.' This answer caused me to fall into the body of a wild fox for five hundred rebirths." Then Pai Chang expounded the Dharma to the wild fox saying: "He does not ignore the law of causality." The old fox was completely liberated by these words.

Even when you have reached Buddhahood you still must not ignore the law of causality. Pure emptiness is the cause. Bodhi-Nirvana [Absolute Nirvana] is the result.

7:30-8:00 PM: Tenth Period

Master: Today your legs were the biggest problem, but after the pain is over—what comfort! If those who study and practice Buddhism do not make great efforts, it's just empty talk!

We must be clearly aware that the three minds [Past, Present, and Future] cannot be found, but we find by not finding.

Ch'an Master Pai Chang's monastic system had a great influence upon the whole society of his time. "One day without working; one day without eating," was his rule. When one is diligent, virtuous mind will naturally develop.

One day a monk, hearing the sound of the dinner drum, lifted his hoe over his shoulder, laughed aloud and returned to the monastery. Pai Chang pointed at him and said: "How marvellous! That is Kuan-Yin's Gateway to Tao." After Pai Chang returned to the monastery, he asked the monk: "What did you realize?" The monk answered: "I was hungry. When I heard the drum, I returned for dinner." Thereupon Pai Chang laughed.

Tao is so plain and ordinary! Don't seek for the abstruse. It is right here!

8:00-9:00 PM: Eleventh Period

Master: Drop everything! When you meditate, any posture will do, but you must let go of idle thoughts.

9:10 PM: Discussion Period

Mr. Hsia: Today my legs are still sore, but my idle thoughts are fewer.

Mr. Lin: I didn't have many wandering thoughts today, but tonight when my legs were getting sore, my idle thoughts increased.

Mr. Chu: During every period, I fell asleep. When I was just about to wake up, I would hear the Master's chime ring.

Mr. Ch'en: Today, the Master made us drop everything, but I didn't dare to drop my hua-t'ou. I have relatively fewer idle thoughts.

Mr. Chang: I had few idle thoughts in the morning. After lunch my legs were sore and after I took some medicine the

Master gave me, I felt a little dizzy, and I wanted to go home. My legs and hips were very sore, but even so I felt comfortable. I was sweating all over, and I felt like my head was separated from my body.

Upasaka Lu: I have nothing to report.

Upasaka Liu: Today I didn't ts'an hua-t'ou. I just meditated.

Master: You have seen many states in the past several decades – they are all light and shadow, illusions. They happened because your ch'i was not circulating properly. The Five Aggregates mutually grinding each other give rise to illusion. I should punish you and make you wash down the entire meditation hall. You must know that that which can see the light and shadow is not *in* the light and shadow. Continue to ts'an.

Bliss develops from "Ching," light from "Ch'i," and no-mind from "Shen." Set your mind in your eyes. Set your eyes on emptiness, and set emptiness nowhere.

Upasika Lio: My joints and muscles hurt all over. After dinner I felt better, but my hands felt swollen. This morning, during the first period, I saw myself in front of me.

Master: You are using your mind too much. Your spirit is scattered, and your "no-mind" practice is not correct. Drop that too.

Mr. Sun: When my back is so sore and my legs hurt, I cannot ts'an hua-t'ou. I can't let go of everything. It seems that there should be some other way to improve.

Master: Tonight, try to practice in your old way and see how it works.

Mrs. Fu: Today was about the same as yesterday.

Miss T'ang: Today I continued to ts'an hua-t'ou, but later this afternoon I didn't do it anymore. I was busy fighting with my legs. Sometimes I was half asleep. Towards the evening I had a headache.

Miss Ch'en: Today I laid down my hua-t'ou and didn't ts'an anymore. In the afternoon, I forgot the existence of my body. When I heard the board, I reached the state of no-mind, but after a while my thoughts came back again. I wonder if that instant of no-mind is what we call IT.

Mrs. Yang: I very naturally let go of the hua-t'ou, and my legs weren't sore either, but I still have not conquered my mind.

Mr. Hsiao: I feel very quiet today. Since I didn't make much effort in the past, today I made up my mind to overcome that.

Upasaka Fu: The Master is saying different things today than yesterday. I have been listening with interest, but I'm still having trouble with my legs.

Mr. Ch'in: Personally, I feel that enlightenment is not an easy thing to attain. Maybe in the future I will at least be able to improve the way I treat others and the way I deal with people in the world.

Twice during today's meditation, there was no "I" but only a brilliant white light and I felt very comfortable. I felt like I was suspended in midair. Twice there was red light and then, too, I was very comfortable. As soon as I heard a sound this was cut off.

Mr. Yang: The first period was very good, but after that I felt my legs swelling up.

Master: Swollen legs are a good thing to experience while practicing.

Professor Hsieh: When I calm down, I feel heat throughout my body – very comfortable. I had very few wandering thoughts. I absolutely trust Master Nan, and I also obey him. This morning I felt my body quaking. Then "I" was forgotten, and I recognized the True "I." When I heard the board, I came back again.

Master: Continue to ts'an "How did *I* come back?"

Upasaka Wu: This morning I really enjoyed hearing the birds, and both body and mind felt very comfortable. When my body felt warm and puffy, all idle thoughts disappeared.

Day Three

Master: This is the third day of our seven day retreat. Today I would like to explain about different methods of Taoist and Esoteric practices and so on. There are two reasons that all of you aren't getting anywhere. First, your understanding of fundamental principles is not complete. Second, your practicing is not right. So today I will tell you about this, and you should pick up whatever you can to use for your own needs.

Sakyamuni expounded for several decades. He mostly spoke about "Emptiness." The Wei Shih Sect teaches "Fullness." The essence of the whole universe is called the Tathagata-storehouse. This is the title of all things in the universe.

We and the universe are one and have the same root. This Tathagata-store consists of every physical and spiritual seed. If the Tathagata-store is purified, it is called "the All" [Bhutatathata], and it is like the Tai Chi symbol: half yang and half yin. The yang part is the "All," and the yin part is the Tathagata-store, which also has another name: Alaya Consciousness, which possesses all the seeds. To take the water in the great sea as an example, the waves are like the mountains, rivers and all physical elements on Earth, and the foam on the waves is like all living beings.

The Seventh Consciousness is holding on to the concept of an ego, like one single bubble in the sea-foam. It is also called the inborn concept of an ego. The five senses are known as the Fifth Conciousness. The Sixth Consciousness is acquired after we are born, and it is also called the "faculty of discriminating idle thoughts."

"Hsien Liang Ching" – the faculty of immediate, intuitive perception, or direct, dynamic spiritual awareness – is the interpenetration of the five sense organs and their five objects, which meet without making distinctions [the mind is not moved].

"Pi Liang Ching" – the faculty of comparison and inference – is made up of the distinctions that arise from the meeting of the sense organs with the objects of sense.

"Fei Liang Ching" consists of dreams, illusions, and evil thinking. If we can expand Hsien Liang Ching, then we can use something and not be attached to it; and when we don't use it, we are also not attached. Reaching this state enables us to attain the "All." In the *Chieh Shen Mi Sutra* it is explained like this:

> Eighth sense
> So deep and refined;
> All the seeds
> Like flowing water.
> I don't want to speak
> To ordinary living beings,
> Fearing their misunderstanding it
> As another True I.

Confucius put it like this: "It passes on just like this stream, not ceasing day or night."

What is emptiness? When you meditate you feel clear and bright – your sixth consciousness is in Hsien Liang Ching, that is, there is no discrimination. Why can you see all kinds of light and shadows during meditation? The root of the sixth sense and your habit energy actualize the seeds that already exist in the Alaya Consciousness.

8:03 AM: Second Period

Master: Prajna deals with emptiness. Emptiness means to empty out all forms.

According to Tibetan Esoteric Buddhism, it is said that Sakyamuni was reborn in Tibet several years after his Nirvana as Padmasambhava. It is also said that in the early T'ang he went to Tibet and established the mystical system known as the Tibetan Esoteric Sect. In Esoteric teaching, in addition to using mantras and contemplation, there are methods of re-adjusting the physical body. If the physical body is not correctly adjusted, emptiness can never be reached.

They also teach methods to adjust ch'i. Life depends upon ch'i, and breathing is closely connected to it. Taoists say ch'i is "no fire."[8] When in samadhi, the breath slows almost to a stop, and our body is full of ch'i. The modern way to express this is to call it energy.

How does ch'i develop? It arises from "shen." When our meditation is effective, "shen" develops "ch'i," which gives rise to "ching." Then there is unlimited contentment and incomparable quiet. There is also the cultivation of the ch'i, light points, and spiritual energy. These are the Taoist concepts of "ching, ch'i, and shen." In the *Surangama Sutra*, it says that we "fail to realize that this body as well as external mountains, rivers, space and the great earth are but phenomena within the wondrous bright True Mind."

---

[8]"Fire" means all desire.

Cultivating our minds is just like clarifying water in a glass – getting rid of the muddy deposit, and breaking the glass at last. The younger you start this practice the easier it becomes because then the physical body is still in good condition, and the mind is relatively free of pollution.

The root of life is in the perineum. Practitioners can open up their sixty-four ch'i routes beginning from the perineum. When one is aging, practicing is not easy because when the ch'i in the perineum begins to move, it will go downward into the legs instead of rising up. If the ch'i circulates freely there is no problem, but if it stays down low, then sexual desire will arise. Older people must go through a long painful period if they want to soften up the body and open the ch'i routes. If you cannot soften the physical body and achieve the opening of the ch'i routes, then you cannot be perfected [attain Buddhahood] in this one lifetime.

9:03-9:35 AM: Third Period

Master: Buddhists considered the word "renunciation" to be very important. They even have a fearless spirit concerning death. If we, as practitioners, have such a spirit of renunciation and fearlessness, how can we fail in our progress toward Buddhahood?

After the ch'i routes are opened up, we are in the light day and night. But if we eat too much, we get drowsy. If the ch'i routes are not opened the vital force cannot go through. Therefore, we cannot reach samadhi. These are all physical obstacles.

A most direct way to reach samadhi is to close the eyes and void the sense of sight. Abide in this way and your thoughts will also spontaneously be void. Then the ch'i in the perineum will begin to rise up, and all the ch'i routes will open up. Keep on practicing this way, and after one hundred days I guarantee you will have some result. However, it is very, very important that you understand the fundamental principles and practice correctly.

10:15-10:45 AM: Fourth Period

Silent meditation.

10:45 AM: Walking

Master: [*drops the board*] This is it. As for all that "discipline, samadhi, wisdom; ching, ch'i and shen" – they are all included here. If you study Buddhism or Taoism you must set your sights high. Vow to study the Unlimited Way. When you have attained true wisdom and learned the methods, then you really have power in your hand, and life will be in your control. If you can really make up your mind to single-mindedly pursue cultivation and let go of your mind, it is impossible to fail.

However, a true master is very hard to find. The Buddha Dharma is very hard to come across. Lao Tze said:

> Contemplate the ultimate void.
> Remain truly in quiescence.
> All things are together in action,
> But I look into their non-action.
> Things are unceasingly moving and restless,
> Yet each one is proceeding back to the origin.
> [*Tao Te Ching*]

According to the *I Ching*, the Fu hexagram ["returning"] has one yang line rising. This is our new beginning. Everything in the world has six changes, and the seventh change is another beginning. When you reach the condition of the hexagram known as one-yang-rising "Fu," you are making a new beginning. The first sign of this is your ch'i beginning to move, and a great contentment arises. Then you must let go of that. Your body seems to melt: this is true bliss, light, no-mind. You can really master your own life. Then practice being always aware when your thoughts start to rise. The whole wave is water; all the water is the wave. Most people cultivating Tao all stay in the void, not knowing the wave is the sea, just as idle thoughts are the function of the mind.

Pure Land Sect practitioners use their right mind in practicing; a very marvellous method. They practice to such a point of concentration that their ch'i begins to move. They spontaneously drop the recitation of Buddha's name and also reach the state of contentment, light, and no-mind. The light gives rise to a direct perception of the Pure Land, but if you want to "Open the flower and see the Buddha" you must just turn around, because everything is all developed from Alaya. This is why it is said that everything arises from mind.

Cultivation is easy – but being a proper person is not easy. You must practice, aware of the movement of your mind, in order to purify your mind. Then you can become a perfect human being.

1:30 PM: Walking

Master: [*hits the board*] There are certain principles we need to know in our daily lives. In the *I Ching*, the T'ai Chi produces two halves (yin and yang) that symbolize universal essence and function. This is very similar to the Tathagatagarbha taught by the Buddha.

The Buddha talks about the Three Bodies [Trikaya]: the Pure Dharma Body [Dharmakaya], the Perfect Reward Body [Sambhogakaya], and the Transformation Body [Nirmanakaya]. The Universe before creation is called Tao by Confucians, and the physical, created universe is called the "Vessel." Again, the Path is called Tao, which means the Way to become a perfect person.

Lao-tze said: "From Tao, oneness is created." What is oneness? "From one, two is created." What is two? "From two, three is created." Again, what is three? "From three, the ten thousand things."

Tao is in the universe. From oneness, spiritual reality [shen] is created, like the sun in our solar system. "The spiritual reality of the void never ceases to exist. We call it the mystery of passivity." The valley of spiritual reality is completely empty, but there is an echo. Its air and light are motionless. "The entry into the mystery of passivity is the mother of the ten thousand things."

Tao is right before your eyes. You should first fix your unfocused gaze straight ahead, and with the eyes half-open very naturally, without force, gaze inward. Spiritual reality is only empty, clear and pure. It shines forth, and after a considerable time, ch'i is developed. After even longer, ching arises, just as the ten thousand things grow in the light of the sun. The sun shines and produces warmth like a hen sitting on her eggs. Shen shines long enough and develops vital force that men and women both possess. If you can retain the vital force, and not let it leak out [through overindulgence in sex, wasting energy, etc.], you will certainly achieve something.

If you feel dull while practicing Tao, you should allow both your mind and body to have some relaxation, because you must remember that after sun there is always rain, and after a cloudy day there is always sunshine again. Until you reach full liberation, you cannot master everything. When you truly gain liberation, not only can you master everything, but you can also remain always perfectly calm in any circumstance. Then you are home.

The *Ts'an Tung Ch'i* says it like this: "shining within the body," which means shining with spiritual reality. In Ch'an practice we say "Insight renews the light," and "I have the Right Dharma Eye Storehouse." You must accept form, but never cling to it. [*Master Nan hits the board – a resounding crack:*] Did you hear the sound of the board? Empty! Empty! "The spiritual reality of the void never ceases to exist. We call it the mystery of passivity." If you only meditate but cannot modify your behavior, you will get nowhere. How can we modify our behavior? "Don't hesitate to do the smallest good deeds, and avoid even the smallest evil."

2:10-2:40 PM: Fifth Period

Master: On the path of nurturing spiritual reality, opening and closing the eyes are one and the same. When your eyes are open, you must be able to not expose your spiritual reality, and also try to unite the self with the light of the universe. It is important to know how to nurture your spiritual reality. You must not expend it too much. You can transform something useless into a wonder. The highest comes from the lowest source. Our physical body is only one part of our total self, so we must not damage it. That is why suicide is a great breach of discipline. The esoteric teaching considers the physical body to be especially important.

Shen is the pure dharma body, ["expansion is spiritual reality"]; ch'i is the reward body [the source of life]; and ching is the transformation body [the Bodhisattva's inner feeling of wondrous joy]. The host is the living light, and the guest is bliss, light and no-mind.

The great Master Yung Chia said in his "Song of Enlightenment":

> The dragon subduing bowl and the staff that
>   tiger separates
> With clear sounds from its two hangers of
>   metal rings
> Are not the fabled relics of some
>   groundless tale,
> But symbols of the Tathagata's
>   precious mace.

Our mind and shen are like the dragon. Ching and ch'i are like the tiger. We must control and harmonize them, because the dragon changes unpredictably. Master Mu-na said: "When you reach the state where you can freely master ch'i, you will spontaneously have super-powers." A true practitioner siezes the true meaning in a sentence. Remember, you can transform something useless into a treasure.

The *I Ching* talks about "change." Buddhism talks about "impermanence." Impermanence is merely the form of change. Taoists speak of transformation. They are all the same principle, but you must prove it yourself; practice and witness it for yourself.

3:30-4:00 PM: Sixth Period

Master: Practicing toward Buddhahood is a great man's purpose. Even an emperor, a general, a prime minister may not be able to achieve it. Virtuous men who study Ch'an also cannot achieve it, because virtue does not mean great spiritual capacity of mind. When we set our mind on practicing toward Ultimate Bodhi, we must proceed straight for the target, discriminating nothing, caring for nothing.

Ancient masters said one can associate with a Buddha, and one can also associate with a demon. Indulging in the joy of samadhi, or not wanting to come out of samadhi, is a breach of Bodhisattva discipline. However, if you are unable to attain this state – the joy of samadhi – you are just wandering around. You excuse yourself for not indulging in samadhi. That's just a lie.

Buddha can neither change your karma nor help someone who has no affinity with him. Before you reach samadhi, it is very hard to purify your mind and calm down. Before the mind is purified, samadhi cannot be reached either. It is also not easy for those who have reached samadhi to get out of it, or to start an idle thought. This is not a lie.

Ancient masters said: "This practice is like a hen hatching an egg." Your whole body feels warm and relaxed, like after you get just a little drunk. The hen hatches her egg by sitting very tightly on it for some time. When the chick begins to peck a hole, stones crack and Heaven trembles. How people have lost their way in their practicing, storing up snow for their food supply, or grinding a brick to make a mirror!

In practicing, shen combines with ch'i, dim and bright flowing together. Don't force it to grow – just let your mind dwell in the spiritual reality and ch'i is naturally harmonized, and even your breath nearly stops. There is only the feeling of breathing out and in, called "hsi." Don't follow outer circumstances with the outward hsi. Don't follow the world of form with the inward hsi. One hsi is the period of a thought. In one thought, uncountable idle thoughts arise. If shen and hsi can be united, ch'i spontaneously stops and the pulse almost ceases, and a great contentment arises. *I* and the universe melt together. The whole body, including the bones, crumbles and softens. At this time, one very seldom has any idle thoughts.

Don't think idle thoughts! Only One Mind, clear and pure! The thousand ways return to One. Where is the One? It isn't inside, outside or in between. We just call it the One. It is inner clarity. When young people practice, what a great advantage they have! Lao-tze asked: "Can you concentrate on your breathing to become as an innocent babe?" In that state, all you possess is that calm and peaceful mind.

Where is Tao? Taoists say it is in the "Ming-kung" – a vital point – and esotericists speak of ch'i routes, both of which are created by Alaya. If your mind is not pure and clear, there will be many obstacles.

When you are practicing, that which knows the environment is the lively, bright Nature. The living bright Nature has no head, no tail, no form. Whether or not you can cultivate mind and body together is all up to you.

4:56-5:26 PM: Seventh Period

Master: Taoists use the eight trigrams to explain Tao. "Heaven and Earth in their proper places" represents time and space. "The trigrams shan (☶) and tse (☱) are connected in ch'i. Thunder (☳) and wind (☴) are mutually influenced." There is thunder from earth in the period between winter and spring. After this, ch'i arises and farmers begin to plant their crops.

"Water ($\equiv\!\equiv$) and fire ($\equiv\!\equiv$) do not interrelate." In order to harmonize them, they must be reversed. It is then known as following the natural course to procreate life. If you have the ability to go against the natural course, you can create an immortal.

Idle thoughts have the nature of fire. Before ching and ch'i are formed, there is water[9] at the perineum, but it has no form. If your mind rests, ch'i with the nature of "ch'i before the formation of the universe" naturally arises. If we can reach the level represented by the Chi Chi Hexagram ["after completion"], then we can return to the essence and restore our origin.

The four Hsiang[10] and the Five Elements all relate to earth, because earth is the fundamental center. "Wu Chi" [earth in the five elements] represents our stomach and digestive system, along with the center "Kung" ch'i point. When the mind is purified, these are also true earth. The Nine Houses and Eight Trigrams, on the other hand, depend on Jen [water] for their nature. The nature of true water is void, without form. Everything in the world that grows depends upon the nature of water. Water also occupies more space on our globe than land.

Before ching, ch'i and shen arise, they are known as potential energy, which comes from the perineum. Thus the perineum is called the source of living water. If your mind is pure and clear, lively and bright, you are aware of a bath of sweet ambrosia flowing inside, from the top of your head down. Concentrate and understand particulars, and thus understand the greater principles. If you just play around with this and that, you will never accomplish anything.

In the mountain, a clear stream arises, but as it flows out of the mountain, it becomes dirty. Get to work quickly while we're still on the mountain!

---

[9]This means there is a potential with the nature of Water at the perineum.
[10]In the *I Ching*, four, two-line diagrams of yang and yin lines.

Everything in the world has vibrations that mutually influence each other. On the earth, as the first yang element arises, we have Tung Chih. When the first yin element rises, we have Hsia Chih[11]. Water in a well is warm in winter and cool in summer. When heat from the perineum shoots upward to the top of the body, it may give you a headache, but just disregard it. Don't try to force or lead the flow of ch'i. Just purify and clarify your mind and this ch'i will automatically return down to the perineum.

You young people should have great ambition. Start from the Confucian standard of being a person. Chang Tsai said:

> For the Universe, establish Mind,
> For humanity, establish life.
> For the ancient Sages, continue their studies.
> For future generations, establish peace.

Great study interrelates all knowledge to acquire complete understanding. If you are determined to spend your life on Tao, fame cannot move your mind. If you want to spend your life on fame, then wealth and honor will not move your mind. So you must work from a tough sincerity of action.

What we call "great learning" is learning how to be a great person, as well as how to be a proper human being. In the *Great Learning* it says: "Illuminate illustrious virtue." Virtue possesses substance and function; "to illuminate illustrious virtue" is like enlightenment in Ch'an Buddhism. The *Great Learning* also says, "Renovate the people." This means benefit others. And the *Great Learning*

---

[11]Tung Chih is a festival of the eleventh month; Hsia Chih is a festival of the fifth month. According to the Chinese lunar calendar, there are 24 festivals each year—2 in each month. The first month of the year is approximately February according to Western calendars. Therefore, the fifth month is around June, and the eleventh month approximately December. *Tung* means "winter"; *Hsia* means "summer"; *Chih* means "arriving." Thus, Tung Chih is a festival for the winter solstice, and Hsia Chih celebrates the summer solstice. These two festivals are important in Chinese society, as they establish the farming schedules, and many other social activities are timed around them.

says, "Rest in the highest excellence." The "highest excellence" is the middle way, but if you act upon the highest excellence in order to be recognized, even though your acts are good, they should not be rewarded. If you do virtuous deeds and you want everyone to know it, they are not true virtuous acts.

The next part of the *Great Learning* teaches gradual cultivation. "Knowing the point at which to stop, then there is samadhi." What Confucianism calls desire is actually idle thoughts. If you can stop at oneness, stop at clear purity, then after a while you reach samadhi. "And that being reached, a calm unperturbedness may be attained to." Both body and mind can reach a calm that is close to Ch'an. "To that calmness there will succeed a tranquil repose." This repose is serenity even in poverty, and resting content in Tao. When not tempted by outer circumstances, the mind and body are calm and content— the contentment of Yen Hui. "In that repose there may be careful deliberation [expedient wisdom], and that deliberation will be followed by the attainment of the desired end"—the attainment of illuminated illustrious virtue.

8:45 PM: Discussion Period

Upasaka Huang: Please elaborate on the ts'an hua-t'ou method!

Master: You had better use a double method. Practice both Pure Land and Ch'an methods.

Mr. Hsia: Today my head feels very tight.

Mr. Lin: During the afternoon my face felt very hot.

Mr. Chu: Today when I woke up there was a block of emptiness.

Mr. Ch'eng: Twice during this afternoon's meditation I felt very good.

Mr. Chang: My back aches. After dinner I felt really heavy.

Master: Now, now. Just meditate carefully. Wisdom can only be gained through dhyana.

Upasaka Lu: I hope we can eliminate the afternoon snack so we can do one more meditation.

Master: Just manage yourself more strictly. Don't relax.

Mr. T'ang: During meditation I had very few idle thoughts. I went out once during the afternoon and I could still keep my mind like in meditation. I personally feel I've made some progress.

After I took some medicine the Master gave me, I felt a great change. I didn't focus my eyes on anything and my ch'i settled way down. I couldn't even feel my hands and feet, but my mind was very calm, and yet very bright, vivid and clear. Every sound was very very clear. After meditation I felt clear and comfortable, but I was bothered a little by the wind.

Master: Don't expect this state to return again, because states change every day.

Professor Chang: The first meditation today was very good. I reached a state where I was completely unaware of my own existence. It wasn't so good after breakfast, however, so I feel rather ashamed of myself. During the afternoon, I didn't focus my eyes on anything, and I also emptied everything out.

Upasika Liu: Today during meditation I was full of idle thoughts – then they unexpectedly disappeared during walking meditation, while I was listening to the Master.

Mr. Chin: The first meditation after breakfast I had no feeling in my hands. During meditation, after four o'clock, my back felt hot all the way up to my neck.

Mrs. Fu: Even though I was meditating well, I felt as if my arms and legs were pulled into my body. I wanted to come out of meditation, but I couldn't, so I continued to meditate for a while. I had to use a lot of effort to come out.

Miss T'ang: My ch'i rose up to make my head swell and hurt. But idle thoughts also lessened.

Master: Next time you feel a serious pain in your head, you must tell me. Don't just try to endure it.

Mrs. Yang: I didn't understand what the Master was talking about today at all. I can't make any use of it. All I did was just to try to calm down.

Mr. Hsiao: My legs are getting better. I hope I can meditate more.

Upasaka Fu: I didn't have many idle thoughts and I didn't feel drowsy either, like sun shining on me in winter. I feel some progress.

Mr. Yang: The three morning meditations were very good except my knees felt puffy.

Professor Hsieh: When my thoughts arose, I didn't follow them.

Mr. Hsiang: In the afternoon I used the method known as "Returning the light inward to the body." I felt high, but it wasn't as good as yesterday.

Master: Yesterday we were close to Ch'an. Today we are close to Tao. [*Everyone laughs.*]

Day Four

第四天

6:35-7:05 AM: First Period

Master: "To purify one's own mind; that is the whole teaching of Buddha." From the beginning stages of practice until you are complete is all just this. Your understanding must be true, and you must go by the main road. The minds of living beings are full of curiosity. People don't know that the ordinary is Tao. Those who study Buddhism must have a third eye—Wisdom—in their heads. The ordinary mind is Tao, and speaking of genuine Tao, it is very difficult to master the mind. If you search for Tao outside the mind, that is heresy.

In Buddhist practice, discipline is very important. Discipline is not for regulating other people, but is the scale that regulates our own body and mind. If you live by discipline, samadhi develops. If you develop samadhi, wisdom develops.

We must act for several decades just as we do in any one day—just as we do during these seven days when we check ourselves on every detail of our own body, speech and thought. Don't indulge them. A demon and a Buddha possess the same superphysical powers, but the difference is in their minds. Those who practice the Mahayana Bodhisattva Way must first eliminate pride from their minds. If you don't want to work hard, but just expect the Master to give you some secret method, you will never achieve anything.

If discipline, samadhi and wisdom are insufficient, it is because of ignorance. Pride develops from knowledge – and when your understanding is not clear, this is ignorance. If you are full of book knowledge, but you cannot apply it to your actions, this is also ignorance. When wrong desire, resentment, ignorance, pride and suspicion all disappear, you become compassionate and serene.

The ordinary mind is Tao! In the Ch'an Hall you must regulate your body and mind. Don't indulge yourself! Don't be disorganized. Remember: "To purify one's own mind; that is the whole teaching of Buddha." All of the curious, strange and abstruse things are merely techniques, skills and magic. They are half of the road, not the way home.

Enlighten yourself, then enlighten others – then your enlightenment and behavior are both perfect. People's minds are all different, just like their faces, therefore we need so many methods to guide you to Buddhahood. In the *Lotus Sutra,* it says, "If you want to get somebody into Buddhism, first hook him with a desire." This is also like the Confucian saying: "knowing the skill to tempt people to do good."

The Confucian teaching of retrospection is the same as the Buddhist teaching of purifying one's own mind. The *Great Learning* says this is "being watchful over oneself when alone." Of the six paramitas of the Mahayana, the first three are charity, discipline and patience: in other words, regulating your behavior. Purifying the mind is inward charity. Discipline consists of form and nature. The *form* of discipline is outward behavior. The *nature* of discipline is when the mind is stopped – so of course there is no desire for evildoing. Patience also consists of inner and outer aspects. It can be divided into outer patience – behavior – and inner patience – no intention of patience [that is, no mind].

While you are meditating, you can calm down, but after you leave your seat you can't. Real dhyana exists all the time and everywhere. If you can be in dhyana anytime and anywhere, then wisdom can be developed. In practicing we must cultivate along a parallel track of good fortune and wisdom. Prajna is wisdom and charity is practicing good fortune. If we can purify our mind anytime and everywhere, that is great Dhyana.

After Ch'an Master Yung Ming Shou was enlightened, he still recited Buddha's name – this is a good example of the double track of Ch'an and Pure Land in practice. During meditation, recite Buddha's name. Chant it slowly. Empty the mind between one recitation and the following one until your idle thoughts arise, then again recite "Namo Amitofo." Empty the mind for as long as you can. This is called the double track of Ch'an and Pure Land cultivation. It is also known as the double track of the void and manifestation. This is an extremely outstanding method, but its Tao is very ordinary. Don't underestimate it.

The yoga method is silent recitation, but chanting aloud can prolong life. Amitofo means infinite light, infinite life. If you recite properly there will naturally be light. Breathing will naturally slow down and ch'i should be adjusted very softly and regularly. What you chant is Amitofo, but the empty part is the Amitofo of self nature.

8:45-9:15 AM: Second Period

[*During this period everyone follows Master Nan, chanting Amitofo. After a while, many people begin to cry and feel very moved. Throughout this period the master is very serious and unyielding. No one dares even the slightest self-indulgence.*]

9:15 AM: Walking

Master: If you recite Buddha's name for a long time while practicing the double track of Ch'an and Pure Land, you will cry. This is because your compassion develops. Empty it out so you won't get involved with the demon of compassion. Don't think idle thoughts! "To purify one's own mind; that is the whole teaching of Buddha."

Mr. Lin! Do you have anything in your mind?

Mr. Lin: Nothing.

Master: Where are you?

Mr. Lin: Here.

Master: The answer is right. Too bad it's not IT. Chang Tze Yang said:

> In the mind, contemplate;
>   Searching for Original Mind.
> When both minds disappear,
>   True Mind appears.
> The True Mind illuminates the Three Worlds;
> Heresy and evil demons dare not approach.

The Sixth Patriarch said:

> In essence there is not a thing.
> On what then can dust gather?

It is so clear — what's the matter with you? Can't you understand? IT is just this. Now you are looking just the way you should during a training. Idle thoughts spontaneously rest! When they are at rest, that is Bodhi.

All kinds of cultivation and all methods are here for the purpose of making you let go of your idle thoughts. When sitting, you do not know you are sitting; walking, you do not know you are walking. Swing your hands! Lin! Don't hold on too hard! Let go, let go! Drop the "let go," too.

"In essence there is not a thing." If you hold onto "not a thing," you are already stuck to it. Yung Chia said:

When not a single thing can be perceived,
   This is Tathagata;
And only then can one be called
   a Sovereign Regarder.

Open your eyes! Purity and clarity. This period is so clear and pure, all in the Pure Land. When the mind is pure and clear, the Buddha Land is also pure and clear. Why practice? Idle thoughts spontaneously at rest. Get them completely stopped, completely at rest. Don't play with your idle thoughts. Drop it! IT is right here. Walk! [*A pause, then the Master hits the board.*]

Walking is just moving your two legs. Your mind is not moving. While talking, your mouth is moving; your mind isn't. It's by nature very pure and clear. If you think there is something that is always unmoving, that is wrong again. All sounds, all forms and all movement and stillness are all empty and false. Your ordinary mind is Tao. If you want to look for something strange and wonderful, all right. Spend all of three aeons looking for it.

Sudden illumination is just this: *Chi-feng* like a knife, *Chuan-yu* to make you turn away from where you are stuck. At such a moment, you are suddenly enlightened right there. There is nothing strange about it. Don't take anything out of context – you must understand the whole.

Let go! Let go! Don't play around with your idle thoughts. If you think there is a *something* or that there is some *reason*, you are wrong. After you reach enlightenment, you will be very calm, kind and serene in your daily dealings. Nothing strange about that. If you're looking for strange and marvellous things, that is "monsterism," not Buddhism.

9:45-10:15 AM: Third Period

Master: Let go! Drop it! A clear and pure mind! "To purify one's own mind; that is the whole teaching of Buddha." Why can't you hear it? T'ang and Sung Ch'an masters taught with "chi-feng." They scolded people all day long. They didn't make it easy for the student. But, after the Sung, masters were all like kindly old grandmothers.

[*The Master appoints three people, Mr. Nieh, Mrs. Fu and Mr. Yang to try to explain the Heart Sutra. Mr. Nieh and Mr. Yang explain it word by word:*]

Mr. Nieh: "Kuan Tze Tsai P'u Sa." The most important word here is "kuan" – "illuminate." "Tze tsai p'u sa" – free, liberated Bodhisattva – is mind. "Practice profound Prajna-paramita" means to be in samadhi constantly. Then one may "illuminate the Five Aggregates and perceive that they are non-existent " – form is void. You "enter the stream of dharma nature, detached from everything." You are then in the stream of dharma nature.

Mrs. Fu: When we contemplate our original nature – that is Bodhisattvahood. In the essence there are no six organs of sense, six objects of the senses, or "eighteen realms." That is the Bodhisattva state.

Mr. Yang: During the third period I felt very good: looking and listening, not looking and not listening. In the *Heart Sutra* the important word is "chao" – illumination. Attainment is "kuan" – contemplation. When we use a flashlight to search for food, for instance, that is like illumination. The great sun rising is like Kuan. The body and mind both vanish. There is no trouble and no pain, thus delivering us from all distress and suffering.

But if you realize emptiness, that means you see the essence but not the function. Therefore it says: "Form does not differ from the void, and the void does not differ from form." Thus to remain in a state of emptiness is form [clinging]. Furthermore, if you can reach the state of chao but have no concept of chao, that is to be tze ts'ai – unfettered.

When we talk about the void, most people feel there is nothing there, which falls into false emptiness. Most people think that nothingness is emptiness and fall into manifestation, into permanence. Emptiness means to empty out all forms. Forms all are empty, but the nature is not. Break time and space, then heaven and earth and I are all of one root; the ten thousand things and I are One. Begin to practice from the point where you have seen your nature. Then going back into the world you can do things to help people without hindrance,...final nirvana.

Where is nirvana? It is right here. After you see your self nature, then you can help the world, help people. Even though you are living in a confused, busy world, your mind will never be moved.

11:14-11:44 AM: Fourth Period

Master: Ch'an Buddhism talks about deliverance. It means deliverance by wisdom. "There is no wisdom, no gain." There is absolutely nothing we can gain. Even if you empty to the absolute limit, you can only see the emptiness, not its manifestation. After you reach ultimate clarity and purity, both emptiness and fullness are perfect. Then your mind can change physical form. That is the same as Tathagata. Fu Ta Shih said:

> There is a thing preceding Heaven and Earth
> It has no form and is in essence still and void.
> It can master all things in this world
> And follows not the four changing seasons.

We must definitely work on the mind method. We must completely understand the interrelated meaning of the whole and not take things out of context.

1:35-2:05 PM: Fifth Period

Silent meditation.

2:05-2:35 PM: Walking

Master: [*hits the board*] This is Kuan Yin's Gateway to Tao. The *Surangama Sutra* says, "Motion and stillness are both unborn." Wild geese fly across the sky, but not a trace can be found. Tao is everywhere. It is easy to practice Tao, but to practice Ch'an is very difficult.

Luo P'u asked the monk Chia Shan: "If you reach a state where there is no Buddha and no demon, then what?" The answer: "A candle lights up a thousand li. In a dark room even an old monk will be deluded."

This is the place "where there is no Buddha and no demon." What do you think? Where is it? It is right here. While I am talking and you are listening – this is the place where there is no Buddha and no demon. If there is a Buddha in your mind, there's a Buddha. If there's a demon in your mind, it's a demon. Chia Shan also said:

Before your eyes there is no Dharma
There is Mind before your eyes.
It is not the Dharma before you there.
It cannot be reached by ears and eyes.

Ts'an! Walk! Don't use your mind to ts'an – how can you make comment on it?

Master Fu was an avatar of Maitreya. His expounding the dharma was like clouds or rain showers. Once he expounded the *Diamond Sutra* for Emperor Liang Wu Ti. As soon as he had ascended to his seat, the Master knocked the table once with a ruler and descended from his seat. That which is able to know, to think and to move – that's IT! [*Now Master hits the board.*] Do you hear? That which is able to hear is IT!

Before your eyes there is no Dharma.
There is Mind before your eyes.
It is not the Dharma before you there.
It cannot be reached by ears and eyes.

An ancient master said:

If only I had known that the light is fire,
The meal would have been cooked long ago.

Fu Ta Shih said:

The handless hold the hoe
The pedestrian walks, riding on a buffalo.
A man passes over the bridge,
The bridge, not the water, flows.

What is this? If you can "illuminate the Five Aggregates and perceive that they are void," *then* you know. Someone said Fu Ta Shih's poem only speaks of the dharma body, not about function. Tao is in ordinary places, in everday living. Even if you're busy every day from morning to night, keep your mind void, but you must "illuminate the Five Aggregates and perceive that they are void." Master Han Shan's poem from the T'ang Dynasty says:

My mind is like the autumn moon
Bright and pure in the green lake,
Nothing can compare with such purity,
How can I describe it?

Someone said that Master Han Shan's poem only talks about essence. Another poem illustrates function:

My mind is like a lantern
Brightly illuminating within and without.
Yes, there is a comparison:
The sun rising in the East tomorrow morning.

When you hear all kinds of sound you should not be attached to anything; not to void, not even to oneness. That is how we must practice. Continue in this way and this is Kuan Yin's Gateway to Tao. In other words, don't concentrate on inside, outside, or in between and you will be spontaneously clear and pure.

2:40-3:10 PM: Sixth Period

Master: Manjusri Bodhisattva truly admired Kuan Yin's method, and in the *Surangama Sutra* said: "This is a true teaching method: clarity and purity through sound and hearing."

In the world, the function of the ear is especially sharp. Therefore, if you cultivate according to Kuan Yin's method of hearing, it will be very easy to accomplish something. In the universe between heaven and earth the greatest kindness and compassion are a mother's love. Therefore, Kuan Yin's Transformation Body appears as a female. It is not easy to cultivate starting from our body, but since the ear can hear in all directions we can cultivate from hearing. That is the easy way for you to reach perfection. When you reach the supernatural insight into the ending of the stream of transmigration, it means that not a single thought arises. But even in this Lohan stage habit energy still remains. This proves that habit energy is the hardest thing to get rid of.

> Before your eyes there is no Dharma
> There is mind before your eyes.
> It is not the Dharma before you there
> It cannot be reached by ears and eyes.

When you hear sounds you should not make any distinction, because you cannot grasp them. When the sound is all over, idle thoughts suddenly rest. Then you can reach the perfection through hearing, which is Kuan Yin's Gateway to Tao.

4:00-4:30 PM: Seventh Period

Master: Mountains, rivers, the whole great earth and all living and nonliving beings are expounding the dharma to you, but you must not cling to the form. Forms of sound and dust come and go, but that which can hear has no form, motion or stillness.

All living beings are originally Buddha. Understand this, experience this. Don't be attached to the form; be aware of it and perfect it. The dharma body is vast, infinite and limitless. The Ocean of Misery is the same as the Pure Land. When you cling to it, the Pure Land is the Ocean of Misery. When you open your eyes and see everything clearly, that is the Buddha's state.

5:00-5:43 PM: Eighth Period

Master: Kuan Yin's Way of Cultivation of Perfection Through Sound is the straightest road from the beginning to Buddhahood. If people who practice Taoist methods have too much fire – that is, heat, tension, pressure, emotion – they should contemplate a bath of nectar flowing down from the top of the head. Contemplate a cool stream of pure water or nectar falling on the head and pervading the whole body with cooling influence. But if they practice the Hearing Method, they can reach the state illustrated by the Chi Chi Hexagram ["After Completion"] in the *I Ching*. This is a secret Taoist method.

> She has nothing to say to her maid,
> But calls just to let her man hear
> the sound of her voice.[12]

Emperor T'ang Mu Tsung wrote:

> Blowing softly from the South
> the wind of summer

---

[12]From a T'ang Dynasty popular song.

Lio Kung Chuan replied:

> At the corner of the palace
> feel the cool breeze!

When we are in the noisy world, the method of hearing is the best one to practice. It really offers unlimited benefit.

7:43-8:13 PM: Ninth Period

Silent meditation.

8:30 PM: Discussion Period

Upasaka Huang: I personally can somewhat control my wrong desires and ignorance. I have already got rid of the desire for wealth, sex and fame, but I still desire sleep. I have used the method of purifying my mind to regulate my behavior so I make fewer mistakes. My illnesses and misery are also less, and so is pain during medication. I am ashamed that I still have wandering thoughts.

Today the first period was comparatively better. After lunch, during the third and fourth periods, I couldn't help myself and wandering thoughts came up. I handled it by reciting Buddha's name and counting my breath, then used the Kuan Yin Way of Perfection Through Hearing that the Master taught us. The second period after dinner I didn't have any idle thoughts. Reciting the Ta Pei Mantra to cure my rheumatism has produced some results. From now on I will certainly act according to Master Nan's instructions to practice the double track method of Ch'an and Pure Land cultivation.

Mr. Hsia: Today I really began to know how to work hard. My mind feels quite stuffy.

Mr. Lin: I worked very carefully today. When Master Nan chanted Buddha's name I unconsciously followed him. My voice changed, my hands were numb, and idle thoughts could not arise. I was in that state for several periods, but later on it wasn't so good.

Master: Very good, but persevere in reciting Buddha's name. If you have idle thoughts, just disregard them.

Mr. Chu: There was a cool feeling coming down from my head, and no more wandering thoughts. Later in the afternoon it wasn't that good anymore.

Mr. Ch'en: In the afternoon, during the fourth period when I was following the Master reciting Buddha's name, I couldn't help myself and I wept. In the afternoon, after I used the Kuan Yin method, I felt much better. Sometimes there is an image before my eyes. During the third period my body was swaying a little.

Mr. Chang: I am really grateful that the Master forced me to come. In the afternoon I followed the Master reciting Buddha's name. When I heard somone cry, a poem suddenly came to mind:

> The four seas are not large enough
> To contain all the people,
> But the room is full
> Of the sound of the sea tide.

In the afternoon I heard the sound of music being played quickly. My tears fell onto my shirt. Mr. Yang startled me, and Mr. Chin did once, too, and my pride calmed down a little. In the evening I felt clear and wonderful and my blood and ch'i flowed freely from my hips to the bottom of my feet.

Master: Very good. Don't chat with other people. Keep on working hard.

Upasaka Lio: I feel very ashamed of myself because, although I have learned a great deal, I am also very lax. I experience many things, but I hold onto them. The first day I couldn't get my hua-t'ou on the track. The second day, I gave up – I didn't want to ts'an anymore. Today during the first period, I did my own work. After Mr. Lu startled me with the board, my state was completely different. It seemed like I was enlightened. I felt movement in my ch'i routes and I let it go right away.

Mr. T'ang: Today, my concentration was in a very good state. As soon as my ch'i rose up, my idle thoughts went right away.

Mr. Sun: My mind wasn't peaceful in the morning, but in the afternoon it was good. There was light shining above my head. Sometimes I got rid of it. The point between my eyebrows feels very tight.

Master: Don't cling to it – don't try to guide that feeling. Don't sneeze. When you are not clinging to it, even heresy becomes a true method, but if you're clinging, a true method becomes heresy.

Professor Chang: This morning I was in a nebulous state. During the afternoon I listened to the Master's teaching, but to me it meant nothing. In the afternoon it was not very good and I felt very sad. All my logic and idle thoughts came up.

Upasika Liu: When the Master recited Buddha's name, it felt very intimate to me. I had to hold back my intense feelings. My chest felt like there was a hot flow into my two arms, so when I recited my tears flowed. When the Master stopped reciting, all of my idle thoughts stopped, too. During the afternoon I used the Hearing method, but still had some wayward thoughts.

Mrs. Fu: Today I felt kind of dumb. When the Master was reciting Buddha's name my mind was very calm. I felt as if something inside was trying to get out of my body. It seems I have understood more that "the two forms of motion and stillness naturally do not arise" [*Surangama Sutra*].

Miss T'ang: I had lots of idle thoughts.

Master: What has become of the idle thoughts? Continue to ts'an.

Miss Ch'en: In the morning when I heard the sound of the chanting it seemed like I was hearing a chorus of apsaras singing. In the afternoon my meditation felt very good.

Mr. Nieh: I am very grateful to the Master, because I had never heard of the Kuan Yin method. Today I felt rather detached the whole day. I experienced the void and illumination at the same time, but nevertheless I still feel that I still tenuously held onto something.

Mrs. Yang: When I heard the chanting I felt very peaceful, and had no joy, no pleasure. When I heard the crying, it seemed I was somewhat distracted. In the afternoon I couldn't meditate very well.

Professor Chu: Today while walking or sitting I always felt as if I were in a tent—very restricted.

Upasaka Fu: In the morning during the chanting I felt very peaceful. My ch'i all rose up but my legs were very painful. In the afternoon I felt the movement of my ch'i. Tonight my ch'i and blood circulation felt very smooth and unobstructed.

Mr. Chin: Actually, I have only studied meditation for a few months, but Master Nan told me to come. During the chanting I felt very calm, very comfortable. In the afternoon when I heard the music, I started to cry. The second time I heard it I felt myself weeping even more intensely. The Master told me to go cry myself out in front of the Buddha. I hope after we all leave this mountain we can be different people in our behavior.

Mr. Yang: During the first period my eyes saw and my ears heard, but I felt very calm and peaceful. The second period there was no illumination, but a sort of nebulous state. In the afternoon I didn't do so well.

Professor Hsieh: I felt disgusted when I heard the crying during the chanting. In the afternoon I calmed down a bit and I could maintain my calm while walking, reclining, standing or sitting.

Master: I'm very tired today, so I will give you all just one answer:

> Don't bury your Master's teaching;
> Considering it to be ordinary knowledge.

Day Five

第 五 天

6:30-7:00 AM: First Period

Master: This is already our fifth day. Today we should not do any chatting. If there is not a rule, we cannot make a picture. Put your mind and body in order and work hard. Do not concentrate on your body, however; emptiness is you, you are that emptiness – so what are you concentrating on? Early in the morning, when we wake up, everything is clear and pure. There is no thing – emptiness and you are one. Throw away your reasoning, drop your body and mind. Drop even your body's inner deposits, and don't let anger, desire, concupiscence and pride arise.

What is pride? When you feel you are something special, that is pride. Don't cling to my words – don't play with your idle thoughts....That's right! Let go of every thought. Don't even cling to your present clarity and purity. You young people must especially pay attention. Some of you are too simple and honest. I want you to open up, but you don't listen to me. Instead, you think I'm scolding you. That's really victimizing me. Remember: sincerity is Tao.

The scholar Chang Chuo said:

> When there is not a single thought arising,
> The whole appears;
> When the Six Roots stir,
> The whole is covered with clouds.

All of you must treasure this opportunity, treasure this period of time. What is Tao? Completely empty out even "one mind" – that is Tao. If we talk about knowledge, you should not have any pride. If your mind is not cultivated, what knowledge are you able to talk about? Don't listen to my words! Don't play with idle thoughts. That is the truth. There are only two or three days left, so get to work!

7:00 AM: Walking

Master: Lift up your heads! Swing your arms! Open up your chest and your mind! Let go of mind and body. Then there's a little Tao there. Don't think idle thoughts. Remember you must be responsible for yourself. The Sixth Patriarch said:

> You can only see your own mistakes;
> Don't discuss other people's right and wrong.

There is no perfect person in the world, but if we can just notice someone's good traits and overlook the bad ones, then there is not a single person who is not loveable. Don't only look at other people's mistakes – from time to time you must carefully examine yourself.

It is said: "One grain [of rice] in a Buddhist establishment is as large as Mount Sumeru. If you don't try your very best to cultivate Tao in this very life, you'll have to repay it with horns and fur." If in any single day you don't do any good deeds, you shouldn't eat the world's food. This is the attitude you must have toward being in the world. If all people in the world were like this, the world would be peaceful and harmonious. Don't play with your idle thoughts! This is not fair to other people. [*The Master shouts:*] Let go!

8:14-8:44 AM: Second Period

Master: Sitting there, you know you still have a body. That means you still haven't thrown it away. That means you have no guts.

"To purify one's own mind; that is the whole teaching of Buddha." There should be no joy, no sorrow. Concentrate on purity: not a single thought arises. That is repentance. Don't feel sad any more. If you still feel sorrow, then it's a demon. Look at Kuan Yin Bodhisattva's face – this is what you have to learn: incomparable compassion; unsurpassed peace.

In the sutras it says: "In a position of wealth and honor, it is difficult to turn the mind to Tao. In poverty, it is difficult to donate to charity."

During the Sung Dynasty, the scholar Chang Chuo met a Ch'an master. The master asked his name and he replied: "Chang, first name Chuo."[13] The master said: "Searching for cleverness is impossible. Where can you find clumsiness?" Chang Chuo thereupon had some realization, and said:

> Light overlays the river sand;
> Empty illumination.
> Ordinary men, saints and all beings
> Are of one family with me.
> When not a single thought arises

---

[13]"Chuo" means clumsiness. His name is literally "Clumsy Chang."

> The whole appears.
> When the Six Roots stir
> The whole is covered with clouds.

Yes, you understand, but can you reach that state? What is the use of understanding if you cannot experience it?

> Trying to cut off troubles
> Is only to add illness.
> Trying to attain Suchness
> Is also perversion.

True mind has no essence and no form, and no direction or place.

> Following worldly causes without hindrance
> Nirvana, birth and death are but empty flowers.

Everything in the world is like a mirage. If you cling to a Tao that you think can be attained, that is a demon. Have you reached there? No, you have not. So if we have no rules, nothing can be accomplished. Someone may say that it cannot be got sitting on the seat. What are you talking about? You haven't reached it, so don't boast.

> I have no wisdom to understand people,
> But I have the wisdom to understand myself.

I hope all of you will set your minds to do something that will benefit the world and benefit other people. However, if you have not attained Tao, you don't have the ability to go out into the world and save people.

What is the method to attain Tao? It is to let go of everything. Because you are unable to let go, you need control. If you can really drop it, you don't need anyone to control you.

Go back to your seats.

8:54-9:24 AM: Third Period

Master: *Te* must be added to Tao. Te is your behavior. What are right mind and sincerity? "When not a single thought arises, the whole appears." This is right mind and sincerity. If, for one day, there wasn't someone to guide you, you would really get in trouble.

From morning to night you feel you're really great— who do you think you are?

All eyes are upon you;
All fingers point at you.

"Strength, endurance and discretion are close to peace and virtue" [*Analects*]. You should limit your speech. Even when you taste great success and reach a position of wealth and honor, it doesn't mean much. If you want to save the world, save people, you must do it from Tao/Te, body/mind, and life.

History always repeats itself. The way to knowledge is within yourself. Mencius said: "If advanced to dignity, they make the whole kingdom virtuous as well." Of course there is nothing wrong with this idea, but you must begin from this idea: "In poverty they attend to their own virtue in solitude."

Why do we talk about this during a retreat? In ancient times Ch'an masters and men of great knowledge all talked about this. They were not just always twisting people's noses! But after you listen to what I've said, let go of it. Don't make an effort to try to remember it. Let it go! Your problem is just that you cannot drop it, cannot let go of your thought. You can't let go of your body and mind either.

The Ch'an Sect is mainly prajna. Practicing Prajna is like crossing a frozen river, like walking on a sword blade, wobbling on the brink of an abyss, or walking on thin ice. People who have not reached enlightenment should be like someone mourning a deceased father or mother. Those who have attained enlightenment should also be like those mourning a deceased parent.

Why do those who have attained something so often lose it again? They think they are too smart. After you leave this mountain, continue to guard your awareness and also let go of your mind. That is true detachment.

What's the use of two or three people sitting around chatting? All living beings are all inverted and insane. Now I hope you are all waking up. I hope that one word has truly awakened you from the dream.

10:04-10:34 AM: Fourth Period

Master: The music of the spheres has ceased. Clear and bright: that's it. Stay aware of it. The lively void is your dharma body, but you should not cling to it. If you do, it is not. "All things are empty in form." Do not concentrate on your body. Yung Chia said, in the *Song of Enlightenment,* "Lay down the Four Elements; cling not to anything." If you concentrate on your body, you will be limited by your sensations. Disregard it; put it down!

Where do your worries come from? From your idle thoughts. Where do idle thoughts come from? They are the function of essence. If you have no intention to get rid of them, then your mind will spontaneously rest. Your bones and blood will gradually all be transformed into a rebuilt person. Physically, you should be on the thin side, because you can see that long-lived people are all thinner. It is said that the immortals all have longevity, and all of them are clear and slender. Also, if your ch'i doesn't work properly, what kind of Tao are you cultivating? Pay attention! "Not a single thought arises, the whole appears" – that's it. Let it go!

There are only two more days. Time is flying. Taoists say: "Heaven and earth make a stove and cauldron. Body and mind are the elixir." Put your body in that cauldron and let it suffer and be transmuted. This is called "Combined Immortals and Buddhas Cultivation." Pure and clear of mind, there will not be a single thought. Clear and pure of body, there will be no obstacles. That is the elixir. What do you think? Do you think there is something in your stomach? That must be a cancer! Ts'an!

11:00-11:30 AM: Fifth Period

Master: What is the state of attaining Tao? Listen to my poem:

> Mountains and clouds fill my eyes:
>   such contentment!
> Endless scenes suddenly become new!

This is not enlightenment, but a state that occurs after your body and mind are transformed. One day Sakyamuni ascended to his seat to expound the dharma, but Manjusri knocked a wooden fish and said: "Contemplate the Dharma King's Dharma. This is the Dharma King's Dharma." Sakyamuni then left his seat. What is the Dharma King's dharma? It is purity of mind. Confucians say: "In carrying our knowledge to the utmost, we are able to give full development to the nature of men, and we can give full development to the nature of animals and things." You already understand the principle of the investigation of things. You also understand the original principles and reasons of things. Therefore, you should also understand the Taoist saying: "Merely to cultivate for life, but not to practice for self nature, is a practitioner's first mistake. To practice only for self nature, but not for the elixir [the physical body], is to practice for ten thousand aeons without becoming a Sage." What is the elixir? Spiritual Essence solidifies, and ch'i is concentrated. Ch'i rests and the pulse stops. What I have just said is for those among you who believe in Taoist practices.

1:35 PM: Walking

Master: There is a ch'an saying: "Beat your idle thoughts to death, then your dharma body arises." "Contemplate the Dharma King's dharma. This is the Dharma King's dharma." You see how easy it is, but still you cannot make it.

Speaking of returning ch'i to the original flow, what is the origin? Where does it stay? It stays nowhere. It is absolutely impossible to be enlightened if the ch'i does not open up the central route.

If you set your mind to practice Tao, you will find demons and obstacles everywhere. It is difficult to jump out of that. Perversion and righteousness cannot exist at the same time. The Tao of virtuous people recedes, but the Tao of those without cultivation grows. Ta Chu Hui Hai said:

> A stirred mind is the heavenly demon,
> A stirless mind is the demon of the five Aggre-
> gates
> A mind that is sometimes stirred and sometimes
> stirless
> Is the passion demon

One righteous person can control a hundred perverse ones.

Even a great scientist can't know the great mystery of the universe. At last all he can do is to fall back on religion, like Einstein did, for example. Ma Tzu said:

> This is a place where a Buddha is selected.
> Empty the mind and you succeed.

Be extremely conscientious; cultivate virtue and practice good behavior. Yang Hsiung of the Later Han Dynasty said: "Devils are always peeping into the house of an outstanding family." Wealthy and honored families have always been hated by all the poor people. If your position is high, people without position are all your enemies. Yuan Han Yun said: "In the highest place there is always more wind and rain. Don't aim for the very top."

If Tao is one foot high, the obstacle will be ten feet high. What is the obstacle? Outside, the environment. Inside, your idle thoughts. The obstacle is created by mind. Evil deeds are all created by people. When not a single thought arises, the whole appears. Let it go! Let it go!

This is all idle talk. After you hear idle talk, just forget it. You must control your eyes – don't be looking all around. Where is your true self when there are no dreams and no thoughts? Have you reached enlightenment? Haven't you just had a nap? If you haven't reached enlightenment, your nap turns out to be a waste. Lin Chio Hsien said in three poems:

> Manifest; not manifest
> Empty; not empty
> The bamboo ladle
> Dips up the northwest wind.

· · ·

> No singing birds in the tree
>   in front of the door,
> Flower petals on the moss
>   in the courtyard.

· · ·

> In the Yangtze River
>   the waves are deepest.
> Travelers all hesitate
>   arriving there.

> If you reach the river
>> at a calm place someday,
> You must still be
>> just as cautious.

Ch'an Master Lin Chi said:

> What is the unceasing flow?
> To speak of it;
> The shining truth is unlimited.
> Separate from form and name,
> Who can describe it?
> After splitting one hair,
> You must sharpen the blade again.

This poem by Lin Chio Hsien is about cultivation.

> I stretch out my legs to sleep;
> Getting up, Heaven and Earth
> Are still as before!

When there are no dreams and no thoughts, where is your true self? Ts'an! Walk!

2:25-3:16 PM: Sixth Period

Master:

> When not a single thought arises
> The whole appears.
> When the Six Roots stir
> The whole is covered with clouds.

When you have no idle thoughts, your mind is pure and clear. Is that "not a single thought arises?" That is only a temporary stopping of the flow of your sixth consciousness. You must let go of the four elements [that is, the body]; drop your body and mind. That is what we call "not a single thought arises, the whole appears."

> Turning the ashes
> deeply, deeply
> There is a seed!
> Everything in life
> just this!

Tung Shan asked Yun Yen: "Insentient beings can expound the dharma. Who listens?" Yun Yen replied: "The insentient beings listen." Tung Shan asked: "Why can't I hear it?" Yun Yen then held up his duster and said: "Do you hear?" Tung Shan answered "No." Yun Yen then said: "You can't even hear me expound, much less insentient beings expounding!"

In the *Amitabha Sutra* it says that water, birds, forest all are chanting "Buddha, Dharma, Sangha." When Tung Shan heard this, he realized something and composed this gatha:

> Strange, very strange!
> Inconceivable that inanimate beings
> Are expounding the Dharma.
> Listening with your ears,
> You will never learn.
> You can only learn when
> You can use your eyes to listen!

This is merely a realization of understanding. Later, when Tung Shan crossed the river and saw his own shadow in the water, he was truly enlightened, and then made this gatha:

> Do not seek it anywhere else!
> All other roads are distant from me.
> Now that I go on all alone
> I meet it everywhere.
> It is even now surely me,
> I am even now surely not it.
> Only by understanding this way
> Can there be true union with the self-so.

What do you say it is? "Past mind cannot be found; future mind cannot be found; present mind cannot be found." Drop anything you have forgotten. Don't try to think of it anymore.

In the *Diamond Sutra* it says: "One should develop a mind that does not abide anywhere." There is nowhere for the mind to abide: that's where your mind should abide.

In the *Doctrine of the Mean* it says: "Tao may not be left for an instant. If it could be left, it would not be Tao." When you say there is a "noplace to abide," you are already abiding there. You must separate attainment and Tao. Don't mix them up!

The Boat Monk said: "Be as a strand of white silk." What does this mean? When you can attain this state you can die sitting or standing up. But concerning Tao – you have not even dreamed of it yet. You must ts'an, "When not dreaming or thinking, where is my true self?" When you reach the state in which "Tao is complete, Mind already at rest: traces of it are everywhere," then you have something. When you are napping, where can you meet me? Where do I meet you? Ts'an!

Drop everything! "When not a single thought arises, the whole appears." Where does it appear? Don't play with your idle thoughts. Don't use reason. This matter cannot be explained by logic. That is why ch'an is "a special transmission outside the scriptures, not depending on words and letters." When your consciousness and thinking calm down, for example, it is only the stillness of the mind. Do you think Tao is that easy?

> Drop the bottom out of the barrel.
> Break the void of emptiness.

That is not clinging. It is a state of complete void. When you reach that state wherein you have separated from your thinking and consciousness, and let go of body and mind, then you are considered to be enlightened. An ancient master said:

> Sword trees and mountains of knives
> are your meditation cushion;

Dragon pond and tiger's den
make your Ch'an seat.

If you let no evil into your mind,
you can exist in the midst of wolves and tigers.

Mencius wrote: "Completed goodness, brightly displayed, is called greatness."
Pay attention to what I have just said!

4:23-5:12 PM: Seventh Period

Silent meditation.

5:15 PM: Walking

Master: [*hits the board*] "Contemplate the Dharma King's dharma. This is the Dharma King's dharma." After the sound, not a single thought arises. Is that calm and peace not it? In the afternoon, yin arises, and if you follow the current of it you will play with your idle thoughts, but if you go against the flow your mind will be bright and you should accomplish something.

In *The Diamond Sutra* Subhuti asked the Buddha: "When virtuous men and women develop the supreme-enlightenment mind, how should their minds abide and how should they be subdued?" Buddha answered: "Excellent, excellent, Subhuti. As you say."

The principle of prajna is very simple. After your wayward mind runs away, it is correct to abide there. Those who begin to develop their minds for Tao become Bodhi. Anything that can be created, cultivated or witnessed is all false. Buddha then answered again: "You should develop a mind that does not abide anywhere." You cannot abide in the Buddha, either. If you abide in Buddha, you get attached to a Buddha-demon; you are tied up with a rope. Pay attention!

The Boat Monk said: "Do not hide yourself in a traceless place." Aren't contemplation and the Kuan Yin Method dependent on form? Yes, but they are only skills through which we can reach the state where "not a single thought arises." All forms are created by mind, but living beings are attached to them. It can't be talked about; can't be spoken of. Don't play with your idle thoughts! Let them go! See what happens after you drop it. The *Diamond Sutra* says:

> All phenomena are like
> a dream, an illusion, a bubble and a shadow;
> Like dew and lightning.
> Thus should you meditate upon them.

Your mind can be pure in an instant! Don't play with your idle thoughts!

5:45-6:15 PM: Eighth Period

[*Free discussion before dinner:*]

A Monk: Are ts'an and ch'an two different things?

Master: Ch'an is dhyana. Ts'an is ultimate participation/ penetration. If you're looking for enlightenment, you must ts'an. How do we ts'an? We must completely penetrate mind by the dhyana method. You can then suddenly and immediately be enlightened in the essence and function of your consciousness. In dhyana, the highest accomplishment is only a Lohan state.

Your problem is that you are greedy for dhyana. According to the principles of Buddhism, this is the meditation on the void – or dwelling on the void – that belongs to the Four Dhyanas and the Eight Concentrations. Meditation on the void can weaken the very strong force of habit-energy, but your idle thoughts are not cut off. Practice from nouan [warmth], to ting [top], to jen [endurance] until in the fourth Lohan stage you are able to master your own death. But ts'an-ch-an is something different.

Monk: Since "in essence there is not a thing," why should we ts'an?

Master: You have to ts'an because you don't recognize the essence.

Mr. Yang: Why did Master Chao-chou still travel around at the age of eighty?

Master: Because essence and function cannot be united, he was not free from the influence of the outside environment. He was also preventing his own fall into pride and preventing himself from losing IT again. [*Master Nan calls out to the Monk, who turns to the Master.*] Reverend! This is it! When the great master Hung Yi died, the Vinaya Sect had no one to succeed him. I give you the "fragrance of samadhi" [imperturbability] and I hope you can take good care of it, and develop the vinaya. Develop great will and do not follow the way of the hinayana. Nothing can surpass this good merit.

Mr. Lu: [*interrupting*] The cause of the Reverend's leaving home to become a monk is to benefit his mother.

Master: I hope so! From now on what method are you going to use for cultivation?

Monk: I plan to go by my old way: "Not a single thought arises."

Master: How do you plan to practice by yourself?

Monk: [*Does not answer*]

Master: I have my own poem for you to ts'an:

> Not expecting liberation
> But free from the Red Dust,
> I am unfettered
> Even in the midst of the world.

> Light above and behind
> Just illusion.
> Clouds floating underfoot
> Not real.

> Year after year peaches blossom
> And spring trees are green.
> Flowing waters and high mountains
> Everywhere bright and new.

> Trying to point out superpowers
> And the marvellous scene,
> The busy man eats
> And puts on his clothes.

When you fold up your legs, who are you trying to save? Yourself, or other people?

9:15 PM: Discussion Period

Upasaka Huang: Today was very good. In the afternoon, when I noticed the sound of the strong wind and rain, I was afraid it was my evil state. After I emptied it out, it was gone.

Mr. Hsia: Today was very good. It seemed as if I were supported by a wooden frame—very comfortable. And I had no idle thoughts.

Mr. Chu: When my idle thoughts arose today, I paid no attention. I feel like I made a lot of progress.

Master: Good. That's a stride forward. Ts'an another day.

Mr. Chang: In the morning I felt ashamed of myself, so I cried. In the afternoon my back ached and later I forgot my body. I saw a Bodhisattva bathing me. After I woke up I noticed my face was covered with tears.

Upasaka Liu: The morning wasn't bad, but I was tired in the afternoon. Then I recited the Chung-t'i Mantra. In the evening, when I listened to the dialog between Master and the Monk, I began to understand.

Master: Today your illusions have all disappeared. That's about right – I congratulate you.

Mr. Sun: Today I ignored the tension between my eyebrows. My nose opened up. My ears opened up and the top of my head opened up into a swelling. I thought it was very ugly so I didn't want to look at it.

It seemed like my body was completely in the sunshine. In the afternoon the light in front of me seemed to be rising up, and it was especially bright. As a consequence, during that period a very warm, strong light shown on me above my right side. It was very hot, and I was sweating. While walking the sunlight seemed to be setting, and I felt really concentrated. Then, in meditation, there was no sunlight shining on me anymore. I felt like ants were crawling on my head and running down my back.

Professor Chang: Today I was very anxious and ashamed of myself, and I worried a lot. Everything was just plain and ordinary, with no progress at all. Something that's different from two years ago is that I don't feel any physical obstacles now. A few times my body suddenly felt very warm, and I emptied it out. I also emptied the white light in front of me. In the afternoon, my legs went to sleep. The Master told me to empty it, and after that I was able to keep that state while walking, eating, or whatever.

Master: When you feel heat again, let it be. Don't empty it out, just let it burn. Don't empty the light, either, and your illness will get well.

Upasika Lio: I didn't sleep well last night, so during the morning meditation I fell asleep. Now even when asleep I am still aware that I am asleep. After lunch I wasn't drowsy anymore. Sometimes I had pain in my legs but I emptied it and didn't feel it anymore.

Master: In your sleep you know there is that which doesn't sleep. This is very good use of mind; you've really worked hard. However, this is not complete penetration.

Professor Chu: In the afternoon my meditation was very good.

Master: Regardless of whether thoughts are good or bad, you must empty them.

Mrs. Fu: After last night's discussion I practiced the hearing method, and I felt very good. This morning, while I was in the yard, I felt even better. When we went in to meditation this morning I heard a glass break. When I heard that sound, I felt even more clear and calm, but after a while I lost it.

Miss Ch'en: Today I felt very drowsy.

Master: In the evening do more bowing.

Mrs. Chou: Today was better than yesterday, but not so good as the first three days. I'm still doing ts'an hua-t'ou.

Master: I hope you will continue to ts'an after the retreat. If you have any questions you can phone Mr. Yang and ask him. Taoists say: "If you don't save yourself during this life, during which life will you try to save it?" You must make a continuous effort. If you can really work hard, after about six months you should get some good results.

Mrs. Yang: I expected to cut off my consciousness today but I couldn't make it. For one period during the afternoon my legs went to sleep. Master told me to ignore it, but I couldn't get free of it.

Master: Don't try to cut off your mind.

Upasaka Nieh: Very simple! I got it in bed underneath my blanket. Today I heard my heartbeat, and my pulse moving.

Master: Not yet. It's still covered by the blanket!

Mr. Yang: Today I was able to find it anytime – very clear! Very bright! But I cannot be certain. I feel that the past four days have not been a waste, but I don't feel I have made any progress.

Master: That you have no progress in attainment is because your health is not very good. Your understanding and faith are insufficient because your wisdom is insufficient.

Upasaka Fu: I want to be able to hold on to my concentration. How can I do it?

Master: You understand the principle, yet when you apply it to practice you cannot hold onto it. Until your central ch'i route opens up, you can't do it. You will be able to do it in the transition period between death and rebirth, because during that period the mind is unified. The *Diamond Sutra* says: "That which is called agglomeration [all manifestation] cannot be spoken of, but the vulgar man has longing for and attachment to this thing." You, especially, are one who must practice dhyana. Once your central ch'i route opens up you can make some accomplishment.

Professor Hsieh: Today I practiced stopping thought and not letting the sixth consciousness arise.

Mr. Hsiang: Last night after I went to bed, I did some practicing and felt very good.

Master: Before you go to bed tonight, I have an ancient gatha to give you:

> There is a Buddha in every mind.
> In the Dharma ending age
> Among the people there is little faith.
> They look for the Buddha Dharma
> Outside the mind, not knowing
> That every mind is a Buddha.

Day Six

Master: Today idle talking is still forbidden.

6:35-7:10 AM: First Period

Silent meditation.

7:10 AM: Walking

Master: When you first develop in your mind the intention to Buddhahood, you then become one. The former is also the latter. From birth until death, there is just this. If everyone could start off being just as good as you are during this meditation period, three days would actually be enough.

Entanglements with outer causes all arise because of your connection with them. If you do not connect with them, they cannot influence you. Be patient from beginning to end. If you are not careful, after a while your concentration will leave you and your learned cleverness [idle thoughts] will come up. You must clearly recognize this. Don't buy and sell IT. Hurry to get it back and keep it.

Why can't you hold IT? Because of your intention to hold it. Let your mind die down: beat the idle thoughts to death, and then your dharma body arises. Why is your mind always so active? There's only today left, but don't worry. Just drop it – that's IT.

The sound of wind and rain. . .people coughing. . .but IT is obviously an unclaimed field; isn't it clear? All these dharmas, all these principles are just old pieces of paper. Why are you holding onto them?

It is very clear – right in front of you, but you never stop. Don't use effort to seek IT. When you let go, there IT is. Let go! Don't play with your idle thoughts! If you cannot calm yourself down, then there's nothing I can do to help you, either. Wind and rain, the sound of birdsong are all just chanting "Buddha, Dharma, Sangha." What are they chanting? [*The Master hits the board.*] Chanting the original purity, clarity, brightness, perfection. . . .

You have finished eating. Now, put down your mind. Put everything down, even your expectation of samadhi. Today is the sixth day, tomorrow the seventh: drop all that! Let go of it! Don't mind other things. Let go, let go! Whatever it is – Buddha, Tao – let it all go. Drop everything. All the dharmas are empty in form.

When all forms are void, you may say, "But I still know I am here." Yes, of course you know, because "Above the Heavens and below, I am the only honored one."

Aside from eating and going to the restroom, you should not take one step away from the Ch'an Hall. If you want to make it, there is only this moment. What is the use of another day or two? If you can't make it, you had better spend ten thousand years cultivating yourself. Walk!

[*Master Nan hits the board.*] You old-timer Bodhisattvas! What can I do with you? What are you going to do? Work hard! Make some effort! Think how wonderful it is to listen to the partridges calling – better return to Amitofo!

The birds in the forest are all reciting "Buddha, Dharma, Sangha" – how clear and pure it is! Birth and death are only transformations of essence, changed and transformed according to causation. You want to empty your "I" – wouldn't you then become a stone?

It is so clear. IT is right here. "I" is right here. What's the matter with you? I'm telling you "I" has no form, "I" is still "I" – eternity, bliss, ego, and purity. It is said: "No ego, no personality." Actually, ego, being, and living beings all have form and no form as well. We ignore their coming and going. When they're gone, they're gone.

8:17-8:45 AM: Second Period

Silent meditation.

8:45 AM: Walking

Master: Don't seek the Hinayana's level of concentration, which is something that can be gained by practicing. Drowsiness is IT! Awareness is also IT!

When the ch'i is very full in a young person's body, the breath can stop for a few seconds [that is, it becomes very subtle]. The body then changes. Bodhi means enlightenment. If you can recognize your ch'i, and it's tight – ignore it. That doesn't mean to empty it, but just to let it be. From morning to night "the flowers fall away – what can I do?" – this is void or emptiness. "It seems that the returning swallows are familiar" – this is fullness or manifestation. "Stretching out my legs to sleep." . . . What are you trying to empty? Everything is already empty in form.

Good! When acting, you don't cling to your action, when not acting, you don't cling to non-action. Very good! That is very courageous. When your wife and children are ill, however, then how will you act?

All the Buddhas and Bodhisattvas will not let you suffering beings down. Don't let yourself get emotional. Who asked you to mind IT? You each mind your own business.

If you want to empty it out, then you empty it out. These are all changes in the true "I," knowing that "I" comes and goes, rises and falls. Above and below the heavens, "I" am the only honored one. If you are aware that idle thoughts are empty, then they are the function of prajna, but if you take prajna as manifestation, then prajna becomes idle thought. Walk!

[*After a pause, while walking:*] It is you who make the mind rest. As it dwells here, it can reach samadhi. You should abide right here, dwell right here. There is a T'ang poem which says:

> Recognizing the East wind,
> Blossoms in reds and purples
> Merely indicate Spring.

9:03-9:35 AM: Third Period

Master: When you concentrate, there is a bright light in front of you, whether your eyes are open or closed. This is the concentration method.

I laugh at myself. I'm just like an old mother hen with both eyes looking all over to see which egg is going to hatch. Then I'll help you to get out.

My words are just like a match I want to use to light your fire, but you don't let your fire light up. You only play with my match. What do you think you're doing? Why don't you recognize the *true* "I"? It is just as Pai Chang said:

> The lively light shines alone,
> Having shaken off the Six Roots.

If you want to tie it up, tie it up. If you don't? Then you are liberated. Here's my poem:

> Why should I recognize the East wind?
> I don't give a damn if it's Spring or not!

This is the smart attitude. Chu Hsi said:

> A square half-acre pond mirrors
> Sky's light chasing clouds' shadows.
> I ask you why it is so clear:
> A spring of living water rising!

And:

> Last night beside the river
> Spring water was born.
> Today how freely it flows
> In the current!

These two poems are wrong views. They only represent the clarity and purity of the mind, not enlightenment. They are only a state of mind. See about mine now:

> Why should I recognize the East wind?
> I don't give a damn if it's Spring or not!

"Contemplate the Dharma King's dharma. This is the Dharma King's dharma." Everything is impermanent; merely the rotation of birth and death: bitter, void, selfless. On the other hand, however, when he was about to enter nirvana, the Buddha said: "Eternity, bliss, self, purity!" Do you understand? You don't? Ts'an! Pai Chang said:

> Essence appears true and eternal,
> Not depending on words and letters.

> If separate from idle causation
> It would be like Buddha.

All we've been saying about emptiness and fullness is really meaningless. Well then, outside there is water running, expounding to you. If your mind is clear and pure, the environment is also clear and pure. If your mind is not clear and pure, neither is the outer environment. Be aware that you are full to the brim. Before your life ends, you must perfect it. In the *Lotus Sutra* it says: "All the Dharmas from the Origin are in the form of Nirvana." Mountains, light, water, color, birds singing, flowers falling; all are in original nirvana. If you recognize Nirvana, that is a mistake, but if you do not, you cannot be enlightened.

All the Dharmas from the Origin
Are in the form of Nirvana.

Don't play with your idle thoughts! You think you're very smart, eh? But you only use your intelligence wastefully. Why is your mind so active? Don't play around with your idle thoughts. Don't think up reasons. Too active!

All the Dharmas from the Origin
Are in the form of Nirvana.

That is only half right. Where is my completely correct answer then? Well, you wait and I'll tell you. If you expect that what I'm going to say is right, then you are already wrong.

Spring is here, a hundred flowers blooming;
An oriole in the willows is singing!

Do you want to applaud? Why is your mind so active? Where does the form of nirvana come from? Is there a coming and going? It comes from your seven-stringed ch'in! When you hear the melody "Lofty Mountains, Flowing Water," you forget your body. One tone, another tone – mind and body both vanish. You can witness your practice of Kuan Yin's Dharma Gate to Enlightenment. You can witness:

All the Dharmas from the Origin
Are in the form of Nirvana.

Then you can really realize that movement is not moving, stillness is not still. It is very, very clear. That's just IT. If you expect more and more emptiness, there is no more place to stand. Remember there is no form of "I." The ancients were so busy practicing, that they didn't have time to wipe their noses. If only you could understand what they were so busy for, then your understanding would be correct. They were occupied day and night with no spare time.

10:45-11:15 AM: Fourth Period

[*The Master asked Miss Ch'en to play the ch'in.*]

11:15 AM: Walking

Master: When you hear the music and your mind does not follow it, then the sound is a help to you. When you yourself play and you forget yourself, you are in dhyana. Listen to my poem:

> Sound like a valley echo—
> If the valley has no echo,
> What sound is there?

There is essence and function. It can be great function. Applied to samadhi, there will be millions of different states of samadhi. When applied to wisdom, it rises through heaven and penetrates earth. Function applies to feeling and emotion, so there will be sorrow, pleasure, joy and happiness. If you want nothing to arise, then it will be after sorrow, pleasure, joy and happiness are no more.

If you say that you are not familiar with this, well then, you must practice. You will be familiar after you have practiced for a long time. When you have meditated for a long time, there will be ch'an. If you cling to "long," you are poisoned. If you can't remember this "long," you are wasting time. I am telling you a short cut to understanding and attainment. Now listen carefully. [*The Master pauses for a short silence.*] That's it.

I've been talking too much. Go back to your seats.

11:34-11:50 AM: Fifth Period

Master: Open your eyes and you see light. Close them and you see darkness. Light and darkness alternate. That which can see light *and* darkness doesn't.

1:14 PM: Walking

Master: How time is flying! Tao is very hard to get. Let go immediately! IT is right here. There are those who have the highest capacity, and by not letting go, are also right. What should those who do not let go do? They must "first have a sincere mind. After rectifying the mind, the body is cultivated. After cultivating the body, the family is regulated. After the family is regulated, the state is ordered. After the state is ordered, the whole world is at peace."[14] Everything is within motion and stillness, you see. Motion and stillness alternating: that is IT.

Hold your heads up! Don't slouch! Is your mind moving? Let it be. Don't increase or decrease it. There is just One. It is vivid awareness. That which can know is it. The *Surangama Sutra* says: "All states that can be returned to

---

[14]From the *Great Learning*.

external causes are obviously not you." This means light returns to light, darkness returns to darkness; eyes can be removed; nose, ears, body, thoughts can all be taken away. Only your knowing Nature cannot be returned. "But that which cannot be returned to anywhere, if it is not You, what is it?" Understand? Yes, you do. Congratulations! You haven't wasted your time coming up here to the mountain. Any of you who really understand should know it yourselves. If you really understand, open your door. Listen to the firecrackers outside – they are there to congratulate you.

Practice diligently! Let it go! This next half of the day work hard. Keep your eyes straight ahead. See but don't concentrate. Your ears can hear, but pay no attention. Idle thoughts are just like wavering silk threads – ignore them! Gradually they will leave you. The six sense organs are six thieves. If you can properly make use of them, they are not thieves but instead become a troup of soldiers defending their country. They can all help you to cultivate samadhi. All can succeed. The ears and eyes are especially easy to use for cultivation.

That which can rule sits above like an Emperor, but has no position. "That which cannot be returned to anywhere, if it is not You, what is it?" Master Tien Mu Li said:

> Who is that 'cannot be returned' one?
> Flower petals cover the fishing rock;
> Late sun sets, wind moves
> But no-one sweeps them away.
> Only the swallows catch them
> As they fly above the water.

What does this mean? I have a gatha:

> Again, who is it that cannot be returned?
> Vaguely I remember my childhood haunts,
> Swallows searching for nests
> Are the old familiar ones;
> That's why they fly so freely
> About the empty eaves.

Let me make it clear to you why you can't stop your idle thoughts. Why do you always want to cut them off, anyway? Here are two poems of mine:

> The Autumn wind piles up
> Drifts of fallen leaves.
> I sweep them away a thousand times
> But still they fall.
> I suddenly laugh and sit down at ease—
> Let them fall and become ashes by themselves!

> • • •

> For many years in dreams I left the world;
> Where can the elixir of immortality be found?
> In an impure and decaying world
> I laugh and throw away the Sutras,
> Resting in retirement.
> The dragon has returned to the sea
> And the tiger to his mountain!

Now let me say something of value to you. In the *Ling Yuan Ta Tao Ke* it says:

> I will tell you all, from first to last:
> The germ of life always depends on true breath.

This means that ch'i rests, pulse stops. You can master birth and death.

> The shining Origin; endless life:
> Empty and not-empty.
> The Essence contains Heaven
> And possesses the ten thousand things.

I can't remember the rest of it. It's better to forget it anyway, and best of all to forget it all completely.

How can the dragon return to the sea and the tiger to the mountain? It doesn't do any good to tell you. Go back to your seats and ts'an!

2:10-2:31 PM: Sixth Period

Master: [*Hits the board.*] I hit it hoping to enlighten some-one, but the wild ducks have already flown away. It's been six days, and all of you have only just gotten on the track.

To attain Tao is not difficult, but to act on Tao is hard. You think to stop the mind is hard, but it is also not easy to stop the body! Are you looking for comfort? Any posture, if held for a long time, will become uncomfortable. Only when you reach samadhi can you really feel comfortable.

After sudden illumination, there has not been anyone who has not continued to practice for nine, ten years, and some even visit people for Tao and seek out masters for thirty years. Ch'ang Ch'ing, after he was enlightened, wore out seven cushions sitting!

If you really reach that state of no wisdom and no gain, you are Avalokitesvara. A monk said:

Ever since I saw the peach blossoms,
Until now I have never doubted.

It is even harder for you than it was for the ancients to break out of this state from the inside [cultivating as a layman], and even greater. Don't listen to my words! If you do, you are trapped.

Some of the old masters began cultivation after their enlightenment, but the Patriarch Chih-che's enlightenment came out of his practice. You don't really want to practice, but just think about enlightenment. Where can you find such a good bargain?

Some people hope to live in a quiet place where there is no bother – so let them go there and not see anyone, not read any books for seven days and nights and then see what will become of them. I am telling you, it's not easy! People are all afraid of being lonely and abandoned. True practitioners should be able to tolerate loneliness and accept abandon-ment.

3:00-3:30 PM: Seventh Period

Master: People don't seek me, I don't seek them. If you can tolerate loneliness, then you can talk about cultivation. So don't cheat yourself and others!

Well, today it seems you have all made some progress; morning and afternoon. You all have a Bodhisattva face now. Your appearances have all changed. Even those violent-looking faces have the look of a Bodhisattva.

> Above the Heavens and Below;
> I am the only honored one.

Yesterday that monk looked like a dead branch turned to ashes, stooped over; like a pond of dead water. In ch'an we call this "Dead Ch'an" – no vital force inside. Today his face looks radiantly peaceful. He is setting an example for you. [*A pause.*] Concentration. Buddhists and others all practice concentration. The first level of dhyana is cessation of thought. Concentrate the mind to one; there is nothing that cannot be done. The second dhyana is the cessation of ch'i. In the third stage, the pulse is at rest. Ching, ch'i and shen all return to the origin. The fourth dhyana is dropping thought to reach purity. "The two forms, movement and stillness, spontaneously do not arise." What is spontaneously not arising? It is *I*. Spontaneity is selfless. Isn't this very simple? Here is Lio Wu-yuan's taoist poem:

> Through my experience
> I found that life contains no thing.
> Single body, single shadow
> Wandering Chianghsi and Hupei.
> Hawks fly and fish leap
> Concealing that of true interest.
> Green waters, blue mountains
> Are the map to Tao.
> In a deep dream,
> Who awakens me?
> On the ten thousand peaks,
> I see the right and wrong roads.

Every day I sleep in the great mists;
Let men call me ox or horse – no matter!

When you have attainment without realization, you don't know that IT is not chaos within the nebulous One. Open IT up, and IT will fill up the six directions of the Universe. To recognize this is the double success of Tao and Buddhahood. If there is even a minute discrepancy here, it will become a huge mistake ten thousand miles distant.

Today is passing very quickly. Why? Because everyone's practice is right on the track.

4:22-4:52 PM: Eighth Period

Master: Tidy up your body and mind. During the T'ang Dynasty there was a monk called Yin Shan. He knew that his "Nutriment of Blessedness" was insufficient, so after he was enlightened he went away into the mountains. One day Tung Shan and Mi Shih-po saw some vegetable leaves floating in a stream that flowed out of the mountains. They surmised that there must be a great hermit up in the mountain. Thus they discovered Yin Shan. The next time they went up to see him, there was nobody in the hut. There were only two poems left there. One of them said:

Lotus leaves in the pond,
Clothing uncountable.
Half an acre of pine flowers,
More than I can eat.

Since worldly men
Have discovered my dwelling,
I have moved my hut
To an even more inaccessible place!

We must understand that if our behavior in the world is of benefit to others, but the mind remains outside the world, we are truly of Great Mahayana origin. If your behavior is full of wrong desire, your mind is attached to the world and you can never succeed.

My "Chi Feng" style of teaching is not for you to imitate. Some teachers are able, at some special opportunity, to cut off your mind in an instant to let you recognize the emptiness of mind. On the other hand, do you think that cutting off the three limitations is final? No, it isn't. If this emptiness continues like this, you will become Arhats falling into emptiness [that is, clinging to void]. Master Han Shan said:

> Walking among brambles
>   So easy!
> Turning away from the moonlit scene
>   So hard!

Open up and IT will fill the six directions. Close up and IT returns to spaceless space. This is a key turning point. After you have attained prajna, then you have the ability to cut people's minds off when their thoughts just begin to rise. It is easy to save yourself, but very difficult to save other people. Do not use this kind of expedient method haphazardly. I too am not that good – I am nothing.

If you like to teach, I hope you will set a good example. If any of you have gained something, I hope you don't just work to benefit yourself. Those who haven't attained anything – don't carelessly open your mouths.

During the next period, straighten up your body and mind when you sit. Sitting is just practicing for samadhi.

5:35-6:05 PM: Ninth Period

Master: "Every day looking for spring, but not finding it...." But if she hadn't "trampled the mountaintop clouds with her sandals" she could not have succeeded.

The mind is a force, just like the force of the physical world, always in rotation. Why can't you find your mind by using your mind? Because, for example, it is like a light that blinks so fast that you can't see it. Therefore, we must figure out some method to see it, to make hardness and strength turn to softness and meekness, then to calm, then to concentration. We must use all kinds of methods to soften up the mind. Then, we can see.

This block of emptiness between thoughts – is it mind? It is only the aspect of the stillness of the mind. Movement is its function, but in movement it is easy to get into disorder and to become impure. We must understand that stillness and motion are both functions.

The true essence is not in the motion, not in the stillness. In the *Doctrine of the Mean* it says: "No sound, no smell." In the *I Ching* it says: "Spirit has no place, change has no essence." Essence fills up emptiness and pervades the entire universe. It shouldn't be understood by thinking about it, but that doesn't mean it is beyond thought. That which can think is IT. Are you convinced? Every supernatural power and wondrous function come out of IT. If you aren't convinced, put on your sandals and do some visiting of those who know. If you have truly recognized something, how are you going to preserve it in the future?

> Sword trees and mountains of knives
> Are your meditation cushion,
> Dragon pond and tiger's den
> Make your Ch'an seat.
> This is just a Taoist's way;
> When the fire of aeons burns
> He doesn't hurry.

If you want to save all living beings, remember that your wife and children are also living beings. You must also save them.

7:12-7:24 PM: Tenth Period

Silent meditation.

8:20 PM: Discussion Period

Mr. Yang: I have been studying Buddhism for six years. In the first two years the Master spent a lot of time helping me, but I couldn't preserve it, and I had no deep faith. For a few years I read books and listened to the Master expound the Sutras. After I read the *Biographies of Great Monks,* I began to realize that they were great scholars as well, which especially strengthened my own faith.

In the Ch'an school the body and mind are used as an experiment in faith, understanding, practice and witnessing. Today I have finally begun to witness the first steps. I'm just plowing – never mind the harvest! I spend at least two hours at home in meditation every day, and I have never missed once.

This morning I used the Kuan Yin Method and recognized motion and stillness very clearly. When the Master hit the board, both my body and mind ceased to exist. My legs couldn't move. I walked a few steps and then the Master pulled me out of line and made me sit down. Then my hands and feet were numb. My blood veins seemed to swell and expand with great force. I continued like this for two hours and then cooled off a little. During the next three hours or so my mind was so clear that no thoughts could arise. I felt very full and stuffy in my chest. After lunch I sat there sweating and continued like that with no change until our afternoon snack. I personally witnessed the forms of motion and stillness very clearly.

Upasaka Lio: As soon as I closed my eyes there were many illusions. When I opened my eyes they went away.

Master: In the future you must meditate with your eyes open.

Mr. Lin: Is "not a single thought arises" the original nature? When you recognize IT, is that just another idle thought? Is the hearing ear consciousness?

Master: Have you ever experienced "not a single thought arises?"

Mr. Lin: No, I haven't.

Master: Ask me again when you have experienced it and I'll give you an answer.

Mr. Chu: From the beginning my idle thoughts have never been cut off. My chest feels a little stuffy.

Mr. T'ang: I too had a lot of hallucinations. Yesterday during the first period, heat rose up from my feet to my head. Gradually, I could no longer feel my body. Today only half as much heat was left.

Master: Your contemplation has improved, but don't cling to it. Drop everything as soon as you see it.

Mr. Chang: The whole morning I wanted to laugh. While eating and pouring tea and burning incense I felt very free. There were no wandering thoughts.

Master: If you continue to cultivate with a pure mind after you leave here, your future will be unlimited.

Upasaka Huang: During the second period today, heat developed in my abdomen spontaneously. When it got up to my chest it dissipated. In the afternoon, there was one period when my mind became a demon, and I couldn't stop crying. A demon outside is easy to defeat, but an inner one is hard to get rid of.

Mr. Hsia: Today my head, chest and abdomen all felt wooden. Please guide me – was I on the edge of something? Master, please have more retreats to save those who are benightedly practicing!

Mr. Ch'en: My legs haven't been painful since yesterday. Once today my body swayed back and forth a little. When the Master saw it he put his hand on the top of my head. I felt his hand was very hot. My wandering thoughts also diminished.

Master: If you continue to sway after you go home, make yourself stop. When it becomes too strong you can silently chant and it will get better.

Mr. Sun: Today during the third period there was light again. It shone on my head, and the point between my eyes opened up. Then my head opened up. There were no wandering thoughts at all in my mind. Sounds were very clear. Here's my gatha:

> Mind vivid and bright as clear water,
> Setting sun shines through my window.
> At one sound of the board,
> The unformed universe appears.
> Marvellous fullness, true emptiness –
> No need to listen!

Master: Good! With your inner potential you can study esoteric practices. In the future it would be good for you to follow a double way of Ch'an and Esoteric Buddhism.

Professor Chang: When I heard the Master expound: "Above and below Heaven, I am the only honored one," I felt very haughty, very concentrated. When idle thoughts came up I captured them, so they very quickly disappeared. In the afternoon, during the fourth period, I no longer felt pain in my chest. This afternoon when I heard the Master's voice reciting the poems my hands and feet couldn't help dancing. Master scolded me and I felt very ashamed of myself.

Upasika Liu: Last night Master severly scolded me. My whole body was in a cold sweat. Today I sometimes had idle thoughts and sometimes didn't. I neither welcomed nor refused them.

Master: This is only a passing phase, nothing to be glad about. If we were to only talk about meditation posture, yours is the best.

Professor Chu: I worked very hard today. Once the Master startled me. I bowed to him three times.

Mrs. Fu: Today I felt very clear. There weren't too many idle thoughts. Once in a while there was a little silky thread of idle thought there in my mind. I felt very tired. In the afternoon, after the Master corrected the posture of my head, my right side wasn't painful any more.

Master: From today, meditate more, play mahjong less!

Miss Ch'en: Today both my hands and feet were soft.

Master: Because today your ch'i softened. When you go back down the mountain, don't indulge yourself.

Mr. Hsiao: These past few days I have conquered my legs.

Upasaka Fu: For the past thirty years I have studied only the principles of Buddhism. Here's my gatha:

> Depending on body and mind
> I feel like a compassionate man.
> At dawn sudden wind and rain,
> In an empty valley hear the true clarity.
>
> Practicing for years with no distress
> Expecting to find Buddha became an extra mind.
> After six days of bitter meditation,
> My mind has fallen —
> I'll see what will happen tomorrow.

My ch'i dropped down. My mind feels very cool, calm and clear.

Mr. Yang: [*interrupting*] After the Master startled me, I could hear him reciting but I couldn't remember it.

Mr. Hsiao: [*interrupting*] I have an ordinary little poem:

> Before the universe we're all the same: ashes.
> Amazing that causation draws us together!
> Faith is just Buddha — there's nothing else;
> Death and birth — don't play with guesswork.
>
> Kuan Yin saves those who suffer, and
> Wei-mo appears as a sick man — so sad!
> Floating into your ear, the tide sings;
> Again we make the trip back to Ling Shan.

Mr. Chin: Yesterday I went down the mountain. I felt as if I were suspended in midair. This morning, during the third period, I felt like there was electricity in my head, and as if ants were crawling inside my head. I had no dreams last night.

Professor Hsieh: My palms were swollen and I just couldn't practice.

Mr. Hsiang: On the fourth day I lost confidence. When the Master scolded me I wanted to leave. Now I feel that a practitioner must offer up his mind and body; otherwise he will get no benefit. I hope I can hurry up and work hard. I don't want to wait for the next retreat!

Later: During Walking Meditation

Master: The sound of wind and rain, clear and loud – that's IT! That's not IT! Experience and recognize this. You can hear everything: to the end of emptiness, IT pervades the Universe. Do not spend your time trying to get some strange and marvellous thing. The more common and ordinary, the closer it is. It is an unclaimed field. You are running back and forth trying to find the owner. Where is IT? It's right here. Return to your seats.

10:04-10:34 PM: Eleventh Period

Silent meditation.

Day Seven

第 七 天

[*It is before first period, as people are taking their seats.*]

Master: Clear, pure, perfect, bright: it has always been here. Where are you trying to find it? Disregard everything! Let it go, regardless of whether it is something or nothing. You don't even see this!

Such a common, ordinary thing! The Great Tao is utterly ordinary – it's right here. Why can't you see it? After you see it – then you can start to practice. How do you cultivate yourself? Every day you eat, put on your clothes and deal with people, but every day *you* are not in the eating, putting on of clothes or dealing with people.

Watch only your own mistakes; never discuss other people's faults. Be patient and compassionate at all times: that is how to cultivate yourself. After you return home you must steer your mind. Heaven and earth are my Ch'an Hall. Society is my Ch'an seat. There is no one who cannot succeed! Do not relax your vigilance. Let go of your thinking mind.

You all understand motion and stillness. Spontaneity is clarity. This is IT. You must treasure yourself. Treasure the Buddha Dharma and this dharma meeting. You must admire each person's virtue, not his talent. When you observe other people's behavior, that is your incense board [*ie.*, warning]. Other people's mistakes must alert you. You must learn from other people's good deeds as well.

6:24-7:02 AM: First Period

Master: After you go back down the mountain:

> Be in the world simply and plainly
> Step by step, practice sincerely.

You must always keep these few words in mind. Upasaka Nieh!

Mr. Nieh: Yes?

Master: What is there? Separate from eyes, ears, nose, tongue, body and mind; say something!

Mr. Nieh: [*No answer.*]

Master: Ah, what a pity! You made the trip to Vulture Peak for nothing. Don't spend your time studying principles. "There is no wisdom, no gain." The *Heart Sutra* says: "By relying on Prajnaparamita, obtain complete vision and perfect enlightenment."

8:56-9:26 AM: Second Period

Master: "Be in the world simply and plainly." What does this mean? Humility; meekness. And "step by step, practice sincerely"? Compassion and forbearance. [*Pause.*] Something gained can always be lost. I make ten words into one, and that one I don't need to speak.

Now it's raining – clouds of compassion; a rain of Dharma. It's clear and cool everywhere. Well, it may be better not to say anything. We can reserve and nourish our ch'i and shen. When our ch'i is nourished to the fullest, then we'll speak and act. Until we ordinary people can realize Tao, keep this in mind. Abide by this rule: don't talk too much. It is indulgence not to observe this rule.

Anyone who sincerely practices will make me really pleased. In the future you must always think of this Buddha Hall. Be careful not to be afraid, but be as careful as if you were walking on the edge of an abyss or treading on thin ice. Be very careful! Ardently practice concentration! Apply yourself to ts'an and study.

During the past seven days you have all made some progress, at different levels. Each of you should know your own level. Wait until someday someone attains great enlightenment – then I'll give him the incense board. Everyone work hard! Let go of body and mind!

Cultivation is following the current of circumstances without hindrance. That is not easy. All external forms, all clarity, all purity are sharp and clear. This is the Kuan Yin Dharma Gate to Tao.

Recognize this: what is *no birth?* No birth is no arising of idle thoughts or wandering mind. It is merely the non-arising of the mind of birth and death. Let go of all connections. We must be in a state of *no birth* day and night. We call this "patient rest in the belief of no rebirth." We must extend this state. Don't you believe it? Spend three aeons looking for it then!

Reflect on the body your parents gave you, like a tiny bubble in the sea. Don't take this as a reality.

Lay down the four elements;
Cling not to anything.

The clear, pure self-nature is the Tathagata's Dharma Body.

9:26 AM: Third Period

Silent meditation.

9:40 AM: Final Reports

Mr. Lin: When I go home I want to be the best quality person I can be.

Mr. Chu: I want to put together everything from the past seven days, and after I go home I will work hard on my practicing.

Mr. T'ang: My faith has been greatly strengthened.

Mr. Chang: I am now just like an infant. From now on I will start all over from the very beginning.

Upasaka Huang: I had two purposes for participating in this ch'an week. One was to look for understanding and the other was to find proof. On the fourth day I witnessed "purify one's own mind." The Buddha Dharma is just an old piece of paper. I have deeply understood that we cannot look for dharma outside.

The Master instructed us to "Be in the world simply and plainly; step by step, sincerely practice." I will definitely do this until the end. I want to reach a state of fewer mistakes, less trouble. My pride and aversion have already decreased by ten percent. I want to catch up, using the Pure Land Method of practice.

Mr. Hsia: I hope there will be more ch'an weeks.

Mr. Ch'en: When we speak of this, it is not this. When we think about that, it is not that. Not speaking or thinking is still not it. This? This?

Professor Chang: Causation is marvellous! We should all especially treasure this opportunity.

Mr. Sun: I understand that self-nature is originally empty and have also experienced something about the bright, vivid original nature. I am very grateful.

Upasaka Lu: I'm full of bad karma. If there's another ch'an week in the future, I want to be a worker and take care of lights, incense and so on. I want to be a duty-distributor in order to purify my karma. I also hope you will give me a job tending the incense.

Mrs. Fu: I follow behind everybody in exercising zeal and repentance and reform. In the future I want to work hard to learn.

Miss Ch'en: In the future I want to study hard.

Mrs. Chou: I will certainly follow the Master's instructions and work hard on the recitation of Buddha's name to cultivate myself.

Mrs. Yang: During this time meditation has cured my stomach ache.

Upasaka Fu: Here's a gatha:

> Making an empty trip to the mountain;
> Expounding the Dharma on Vulture Peak is
>   wasted.
> If I had known that a nun is made of a woman,
> I could even be a monk at home!

[*Everyone laughs.*]

Upasaka Nieh: After today I will certainly live most ordinarily and plainly.

Mr. Chin: From today on, I have made up my mind to talk less and to discipline myself a little more seriously.

Professor Hsieh: A seven day retreat was worth more than fifty years of study. Getting rid of thoughts is just like farting. If you have gas, you must get rid of it. Why would you want to keep it in? Don't you feel better if you let it go?

Mr. Shang: This time I understand:

> If a man hears the right way in the morning,
> He may die in the evening without regret.[15]

When our ordinary mind dies, the mind of Tao arises. Gradual cultivation is wiping the dust off the mirror – you wipe it once and the dust settles again. Sudden illumination is like breaking the mirror. You don't have to wipe the mirror any more.

Mr. Yang: In the past few years, as my Tao increased, my bedevilment also increased. . .sort of embarrassing. All of you are very zealous, so I have learned a lot from you. This time Master Nan helped us even though he is ill. We should be very grateful for his benevolent, kind and grandmotherly heart. I hope we have all learned from the *Yuan Liao Fan Sse Hsun* to diligently cultivate virtue. As for the mind method, we can only do our best. Mind creates everything. Cultivating virtue – people with money can contribute money to others; people with strength can contribute their strength. Solitary attainment is when no evil mind arises. We must cultivate from the place where mind arises and thoughts move.

---

[15]From the *Analects,* the sayings of Confucius compiled by Tseng Tze.

Glossary

Alaya: The store of consciousness, also called the seed or the eighth consciousness.

Amitofo: The Buddha of Infinite Light of the Western Paradise of Bliss who saves all those who call on his name. Primary Buddha of the Pure Land Sect.

Analects: The sayings of Confucius, compiled by Tseng Tze.

Apsara: Heavenly spirits, often portrayed as beautiful maidens with musical instruments.

Avalokitesvara: Kuan Yin or the Goddess of Mercy in China, so called because of his appearance as a benevolent woman. He attained enlightenment by means of the faculty of hearing.

Bhutatathata: The Real, unchangeable reality behind all phenomena.

Boat Monk: (Chuang-tze Ho Shang) A monk who lived on a boat who was responsible for the enlightenment of Chia Shan.

Bodhi: Enlightenment

Bodhisattva: A Mahayanist seeking not only self enlightenment, but also the enlightenment of others. He is devoid of egoism and devoted to helping others.

Causal Ground Bodhisattva: One who has accepted a cause (Bodhisattvahood) but who has not yet reached the state of attainment, not yet having escaped the chain of transmigration.

Ch'an Men Jih Sung: (禪門日誦) A daily guide for temple practice, containing schedules of Sutras to be recited at services. Includes also mantras and advice to those living in the temple.

Ch'ang Ch'ing: (長慶) A disciple of Hsueh Feng; he began to practice seriously after his enlightenment.

Chang Chuo: (張拙) A Sung Dynasty scholar. His name literally means "Clumsy Chang."

Chang Tsai: (張載) [1020-1077]. One of the most prominent of Sung Neo Confucians, he drew his inspiration mainly from the *I Ching*.

Chang Tze Yang: (張紫陽) Eminent Sung Taoist; well-versed in ch'an. His works attest his realization of the mind. He wrote the *Wu Chen Pien* (悟真篇) in 1073 and his works are included in the *Imperial Collection of Ch'an Sayings*.

Chao: (照) In Chinese it means illuminating, shining. Usually refers to a ch'an master's application of his wisdom to "shine upon" or probe his student's developed potentiality.

Chao Chou: Master Chao Chou Ts'ung Shen (趙州從諗) [778-897]. Taught sudden enlightenment in the southern tradition of Hui Neng while living in Hopei in northern China.

Ch'i: (氣) Means air, breath. This is the vital force that flows in the human body. Combined with Ching and Shen (see Ching/Ch'i/Shen), it is considered most important by taoists.

Chia Shan: Master Chia Shan (夾山) [804-881]. Enlightened Luo P'u; was himself enlightened when the Boat Monk knocked him into the water.

Chieh Shen Mi Ching: (解深密經) Sandhi-nirmocana Sutra.

Chi-feng: (機鋒) The direct intervention of a master in the form of a dialogue, a nose tweak, a slap, a shout, or any other means to help a student reach enlightenment. See also *Chuan-yu.*

Chih: Stopping the flow of thoughts.

Chih Che: Great Teacher Chih Che (智者) [588-597]. Another name for Chi-i (智顗), founder of the T'ien T'ai Sect.

Chih/Kuan: (止觀) A T'ien T'ai method of practice. Chih is the putting to rest of wandering mind or stopping the flow of thoughts. Kuan is looking into, or observing, or insight into the real. The mind at rest is called Chih; the mind seeing clearly is called Kuan.

Ch'in: The Ku-ch'in (古琴) or seven-stringed zither of antiquity. Sometimes referred to in the West as the "Chinese Lute."

Ching: (精) Means spirit, vital force. See Ching/Ch'i/Shen.

Ching/Ch'i/Shen: Ching (精) is the manifestation of vital force in form; Ch'i (氣) or (炁) is the vital force itself; and Shen (神) is the spiritual essence which arises from emptying out Ch'i. Body transformation depends on cultivation of the three.

Chuan-yu: (轉語) The understanding that must follow an experience of Chi-feng.

Ch'u Ch'an: (初禪) One of the four Dhyanas; the first stage in which idle thoughts are extinguished.

Chung-t'i: (準提) A Bodhisattva, the Great Buddha Mother, source or origin of the Dharmas.

Collection of the Wei Mo Hall: (維摩精舍叢書) A collection in four sections recording events and teachings of Master Yuan Huan Hsien; including a record of a Ch'an training in which Master Nan was a participant; collected by Master Yuan's students.

Cultivation: Esoteric exercises, physical training, breathing methods, meditation methods to open up Ch'i channels for body transformation. Also means "practice" in other sects.

Dharma: The truth, law or doctrine; a thing, all things, anything great or small, visible or invisible, real or unreal, concrete thing or abstract idea. It connotes Buddhism as the perfect religion and has the second place in the Triple Gem.

Dharma Body: Body in its essential nature, or that of the Buddha as such; it is perceptible to Buddhas only.

Dharma King: The Buddha.

Dharmakaya: See Pure Dharma Body.

Dhyana: Meditation, abstract contemplation, meditative study of the "mean," which is inclusive of both unchanging noumenon and changing phenomenon.

Diamond Sutra: (金剛經) A major Buddhist Sutra in which Sakyamuni expounded the emptiness.

Doctrine of the Mean: One of the classic Four Books of China.

Eighteen Realms: The six organs, their objects and their perceptions.

Esoteric Sect: Tibetan Buddhism, including Tantra.

Five Aggregates: Skandhas, the five components of a human being: 1) Physical form; 2) Feeling; 3) Discerning; 4) Action; 5) Consciousness. The first is physical and the other four are mental qualities.

Fo T'u Ch'eng: (佛圖澄) An Indian monk who came to Loyang in about 310 AD, noted for his magic; he is also known as Buddhochinga or Buddhasimba.

Four Books: (四書) They are: *The Great Learning, The Doctrine of the Mean, The Analects, The Mencius.* Confucian classic texts that have the strongest influence on Chinese society and government.

Four Elements: Manifestation; that is, earth, water, fire, air.

Four Forms: Ego, personality, being and life; described in the *Diamond Sutra.*

Fu Ta Shih: (傅大士) [497-569]. An eminent Ch'an Upasaka; author of the *Hsin Wang Ming* (心王銘).

Gateless Gate: Ch'an master's teaching method. It means no method is the method. No gate is the gate.

Gatha: A stanza or poem or chant; one of the twelve divisions of the Mahayana canon.

Great Learning: One of the classic Four Books.

Han Shan: "Cold Mountain" (寒山) [627-649]. Said to be an avatar of Manjusri, appearing as a mad monk living in a cold grotto on T'ien T'ai mountain in the Chen Kuan reign.

Han Shan: "Silly Mountain" (憨山) [1546-1623]. Ch'an Master Te Ching (德清) adopted the name "Silly Mountain"; he was responsible for the revival of the Ch'an Sect in China during the Ming Dynasty.

Hand Chime: A small silver bell with a long handle used in Buddhist ritual.

Hinayana: "Small Vehicle" (also called "Half-word"). Preliminary teaching given by the Buddha to his disciples who were still not qualified for receiving the Mahayana doctrines (called "Whole-word").

Huai Jang: (懷讓) [677-744]. A Dharma successor of the Sixth Patriarch Hui Neng, and teacher of Ma Tzu.

Huang Lung Hui Nan: (黃龍慧南) [1002-1069]. His most famous teaching is known as the Three Gates. Lu Tzu, who later became one of the Eight Immortals, was enlightened by him.

Huang P'o Hsi Yun: (黃檗希運) [776-856]. Disciple of Pai Chang and author of *The Zen Teaching of Huang Po: The Transmission of Mind* (see Bibliography under Blofeld).

Hua-t'ou: (話頭) Literally translated from the Chinese, it means "a short sentence," "a few words," "a phrase," "the beginning of a sentence." A technique devised by enlightened masters who taught their disciples to turn the "light" inwards on the mind in order to stop all thoughts to attain singlemindedness and thereby realize it as the perception of their self-nature.

Hung Yi: (弘一) Modern master, legalist and Confucian; a musician, composer, painter and calligrapher, who studied art in Japan, became a monk at forty, and died at age sixty.

Jen: (忍) Calmness and endurance, the third stage of the four developments of cultivation.

Karma: Moral action causing future retribution, and either good or evil transmigration.

Kasyapa: A Brahmin of Magadha, disciple of the Buddha, to whom was handed down the Mind Dharma, outside of the scriptures; the First Patriarch of the Ch'an Sect; accredited with supervising the first compilation of the Buddha's sermons.

Kuan: (觀) To observe, to contemplate.

Kuan Hsiang: Contemplation, often as visualization.

Kuan Tze Ts'ai P'u Sa: (觀自在菩薩) Literally: Contemplate-Self-Unfettered-Bodhisattva. A name for Avalokitesvara Bodhisattva, also known as Sovereign Regarder and Regarder of Sound; he attained enlightenment through sound, or the faculty of hearing.

Kumarajiva: (鳩摩羅什) [?- c. 412 AD in Ch'ang-an]. He was the early and most effective propagator of Mahayana Buddhism in China, noted for the number and excellence of his translations.

Liang Wu Ti: (梁武帝) [464-549]. Emperor at the time of Bodhidharma's arrival in China.

Lin Chi I Hsuan: (臨濟義玄) [787-867]. Disciple of Huang P'o and founder of the Lin Chi Sect, one of the five Ch'an sects of China.

Lin Chio Hsien: (林酒仙) [? -1010]. Sung Dynasty, popular name of Master Yu Hsien (遇賢) who loved drinking wine and writing Ch'an poetry.

Ling Yuan Ta Tao Ko: (靈源大道歌) Sung Dynasty Taoist poems pertaining to levels of practice. Written by the woman adept Tseng Wen-i (曹文逸) as a guide to practice, it uses straightforward language instead of the ancient mysterious alchemical terms. This is the earliest systematic Taoist teaching in writing.

Lio Kung Chuan: (柳公權) Famous T'ang Dynasty calligrapher.

Liu Wu Yuan: (劉悟元) Yuan Dynasty Taoist Master.

Lohan: (羅漢) Arhat, the saint of small vehicle, or level of accomplishment. The lohan lives for himself, without devotion to saving all living beings.

Luo P'u: (洛甫) [833-893] Ch'an Master Yuan An of Luo P'u; at first a disciple of Lin Chi, later enlightened by Chia Shan.

Mahayana: The Great Vehicle, which indicates universalism or salvation for all, for all are Buddhas and will attain enlightenment.

Maitreya: The Buddhist Messiah, or coming Buddha, now in the Tusita Heaven who is to come 5,000 years after the Nirvana of Sakyamuni Buddha.

Manjusri: A Bodhisattva who is the symbol of wisdom and is placed on the Buddha's left. His Bodhi-mandala is on the Five-peaked Mountain in China.

Mantra: An incantation, spell, oath; mystical formulae used in Yoga to control the mind so that it cannot be affected by external influence.

Mantra of Great Compassion: (大悲咒) A mantra most commonly employed by members of the Pure Land Sect, and also often a part of daily temple ritual.

Ma Tzu Tao I: (馬祖道一) [? -788]. Teacher of Pai Chang. He was a disciple of Huai Jang.

Mei Tze Ho Shang: (梅子和尚) A student of Ma Tzu. His name literally means "plum."

Mencius: (孟子) Author of *The Mencius* of the Four Books. Regarded as a sage, second only to Confucius.

Milarepa: See Mu Na Tzu Shih.

Mount Sumeru: The central mountain of every world, also the highest and greatest in the universe. At the top are Indra's heavens; below them are the four deva-lokas (the abodes of the gods); around are eight circles of mountains and between them are the eight seas – the whole forming nine mountains and eight seas.

Mu Na Tzu Shih: (木訥祖師) [1052-1135]. A Master of the Esoteric School of Buddhism, also known as Milarepa. He insisted that his extraordinary attainment was due to long and bitter practice throughout his own present life, starting from the most ordinary roots.

Neo-Confucianism: A late development of Confucianism that took many ideas from ch'an and incorporated them into Confucian thought.

Nirmanakaya: See Transformation Body.

Nirvana: Complete extinction of individual existence; cessation of rebirth and entering into bliss.

Nouan: (暖) Warmth. The first stage of the four developments of Cultivation.

Opening the Flower and Seeing the Buddha: (花開見佛) Final stage of Pure Land cultivation, wherein one can create one's own body at will, assuming any form. The mastery of form.

Ou-yang Ching-wu: (歐陽竟吾) [1871-1944]. A modern proponent of intellectual Buddhism; one of the most influential Buddhist scholars.

Padmasambhava: (蓮花生大士) The Lotus Born Bodhisattva who took the Dharma to Tibet.

Pai Chang Huai Hai: (百丈懷海) [720-815]. Successor of Ma Tzu and master of Huang P'o; known for his Pure Rules for monks, for example the famous "A day without work is a day without food."

P'ang Yun: (龐蘊) [? -816] An eminent Ch'an upasaka who at the beginning of the Chen Yuan reign [785-804] called on Master Shih T'ou (石頭) and was awakened to the truth. Later he called on Ma Tzu and attained instantaneous enlightenment. His family, consisting of wife, son and daughter, all realized the absolute reality.

Pao Chih Ho Shang: (寶誌和尚) [409-506]. Emperor Liang Wu Ti's master.

Perfect Reward Body (Sambhogakaya): A Buddha's body of bliss, or completion of transformation of karma body of the life, which is the embodiment of the previous life's deeds, behaviors, consciousness.

Perineum: Called the Hai Ti (海底), it is the lowest vital point, or ch'i point, at the base of the body.

P'o Ts'an: (破參) A breakthrough state of ts'an.

Prajna: Fundamental, transcendental wisdom that is inherent in everyone.

Pure Dharma Body (Dharmakaya): Body of the truth, the embodiment of the law, shining everywhere, enlightening all.

Pure Land Sect: Established by Hui-yuan (慧遠) [334-416]. Buddhist vow to be reborn in Amida. Buddha's world of purity. Their practice is mainly reciting Amida Buddha's name – Amitofo – constantly, with or without voice.

Sakyamuni: Gautama Buddha, the Sage of the Sakya Clan, born in the mid fifth century BC in northern India.

Samadhi: (三昧) The internal state of imperturbability, exempt from all external sensation; this state precedes the attainment of Buddhahood.

Sambhogakaya: See Perfect Reward Body.

Sangha: The corporate assembly of at least three or four monks under a chairman, empowered to hear confession, grant absolution and ordain. It has come to mean monks in general in Chinese society.

Shen: (神) Spiritual Reality. Means god, superphysical ability. See Ching/Ch'i/Shen.

Six Paramitas: The perfect gift of charity, moral conduct, patient endurance, zeal and devotion, abstract meditation, and wisdom.

Six Roots: The senses: taste, hearing, sight, smell, touch, and mind.

Sixth Consciousness: The faculty of comparison, discrimination.

Sixth Patriarch: Hui Neng (慧能) [637-713]. The sixth Chinese Patriarch, Dharma successor of the fifth Patriarch Hung Jen of the Ch'an Sect.

Skandhas: See Five Aggregates.

Small Vehicle: Hinayana, the form of Buddhism developed after Sakyamuni's death. The objective is personal salvation.

Su Tung Po: (蘇東坡) [1037-1101]. Sung Dynasty scholar, statesman and poet.

Subhuti: A senior disciple of the Buddha, to whom the sermon of the *Diamond Sutra* is addressed.

Surangama Sutra: This important sermon contains the essence of the Buddha's teaching, revealing the law of causality relating to both delusion and enlightenment, and teaches the methods of practice and realization to destroy forever the roots of birth and death.

Ta Chu Hui Hai: (大珠慧海) T'ang Dynasty master; student of Ma Tzu: known as the "Great Pearl."

Ta Hui Kao: (大慧杲) [1089-1163]. One of the most influential masters of the Sung period. The great hero Yueh Fei was one of his disciples.

T'ai Chi Symbol: (太極圖) Half black and half white circle representing the balance of opposing forces of yin and yang.

Tao Chi: (道濟) [1148-1208]. Also known as Chi Tien (濟顛) meaning "Crazy Person." He appeared to be mad, but helped people in many strange ways, such as curing illness. His deeds have been widely used in drama and literature.

Tathagata: One of the highest titles of a Buddha: he who came as did all Buddhas; who took the absolute way of cause and effect, and attained to perfect wisdom.

Tathagatagarbha: Storehouse. See Alaya.

Three Bodies (Trikaya): The Dharma Body, Reward Body and Transformation Body. (See also Pure Dharma Body and Perfect Reward Body.) The three are a trinity essentially one, each in the other.

T'i Hu Kuan Ting: (醍醐灌頂) A process of contemplation in meditation. One may feel a cool stream of pure, fragrant dew descending from above the head to pervade the entire body with cooling influence.

T'ien Mu Li: (天目禮) Ch'an Master of the Sung Dynasty.

Ting: (頂) Top, the second stage of the four developments of cultivation.

Transformation Body (Nirmanakaya): By this body one can appear in any form.

Transmission of the Lamp: (Ching Te Ch'uan Teng Lu 景德傳燈錄) A collection of Ch'an texts compiled in the Ching Te reign [1004-07] by Tao Yuan, in fourteen volumes.

Trikaya: See Three Bodies.

Triple Gem: Buddha, Dharma, Sangha.

Ts'an: (參) To participate, to seek, to study.

Ts-an T'ung Ch'i: Han Dynasty text combining Taoist and Buddhist thought with the *I Ching.* It is very important as a practical guide for practice, especially for Taoists.

Tung Shan Liang Chieh: (洞山良价) [807-869]. He was completely enlightened one day while crossing a river and seeing his shadow in the water.

Tze Ts'ai: (自在) Literally translated from the Chinese, it means "free," "liberated."

Upasaka: A lay brother.

Upasika: A lay sister.

Vairocana: The "Great Sun" or "Sea of Nature." The Dharmakaya of Sakyamuni Buddha; his Nirmanakaya being called Sakyamuni.

Vinaya Sect: One of the three divisions of the Tripitaka (the "Three Baskets" of the Buddhist canon), which deals with rules and rites; the other two being Sutras (sermons) and Sastras (commentaries).

Wang Yang Ming: (王陽明) [1472-1528]. Ming Dynasty Neo-Confucian: author of the *Yang Ming Chih Hsueh*. After studying the T'ien T'ai sect of Buddhism, he formulated a philosophy based on the works of Mencius. His was a system of dynamic idealism in which the human mind contains all things, and to investigate phenomena and action one must investigate the mind.

Wei Mo: Vimalakirti, a lay disciple of the Buddha.

Wei Pai Yang: (魏伯陽) Author of the *Ts'an T'ung Ch'i*, which was the main Taoist text in the period preceding the arrival of Buddhism in China in the Later Han.

Wei Shih Sect: The Consciousness-Only Sect, which holds that all is mind.

Wooden Fish: A wooden drum used in Buddhist ritual; may be very large, or small enough to hold in the hand.

Yang: (陽) The positive, light, active principle of the Universe.

Yen Hui: (顏回) The favorite pupil of Confucius. His nature was calm and without desire.

Yin: (陰) The negative, dark, receptive principle of the Universe.

Yo Shan Wei Yen: (藥山惟嚴) [745-828]. Ch'an Master Wei Yen of Yo Shan, successor of Master Shih-t'ou and teacher of Yun Yan; also studied with Ma Tzu.

Yuan Han Yun: (袁寒雲) Son of Yuan Shih K'ai. Wrote a poem (see page 77) advising his father against the re-establishment of the dynastic system of government with Yuan Shih K'ai at its head, after the 1911 revolution that established the Republican Era.

Yuan Huan Hsien: (袁煥仙) Modern master; a layman and Master Huai Chin Nan's master at the time of his enlightenment.

Yuan Liao Fan Sse Hsun: (袁了凡四訓) *Liao Fan's Four Precepts* was written by Yuan Liao Fan, a Ming Dynasty Confucian scholar of the Chin Shih (進士) degree. This treatise sets up standards for all people to live by. It has four categories: Establishing a Life Principle, Daily Retrospection, Virtuous Behavior, and Virtue in Moderation.

Yung Chia Hsuan Chueh: (永嘉玄覺) [665-713]. Author of the "Song of Enlightenment." His enlightenment was verified the day he called on the Sixth Patriarch for instruction. He left the next morning, and so was called the "Overnight Enlightened One."

Yung Ming Yen Shou: (永明延壽) [904-975]. Yen Shou of Yun Ming, a famous Ch'an master, Dharma successor of State Master Teh Shao. Said to be an avatar of Amitabha Buddha, he wrote the extensive collection *Mirror of the Sect* (*Tsung Ching Lu* 宗鏡錄), in which he linked all the seeming-ly contradictory Buddhist doctrines into one reality.

Bibliography

Blofeld, John. *The Zen Teaching of Huang Po: The Transmission of Mind*. London: The Buddist Society, 1968.

———— *The Zen Teaching of Hui Hai:* London: Rider; 1962.

Chang, Chung-yuan. *Tao: A New Way of Thinking*. New York: Harper & Row, 1975.

Chu, Wen Kuan. *Tao and Longevity: Mind-Body Transformation*, York Beach, ME: Samuel Weiser, 1984.

Conze, Edward. *Buddhist Wisdom Books*. London: Allen & Unwin, 1958.

Legge, James. *The Four Books*. Oxford: Clarendon Press, 1899.

Luk, Charles. *Ch'an and Zen Teaching, Series I*. London: Rider, 1960.

———— *Ch'an and Zen Teaching, Series II*. London: Rider, 1966.

———— *Ch'an and Zen Teaching, Series III*. London: Rider, 1969.

———— *Surangama Sutra*. London: Rider, 1973.

Reps, Paul. *Zen Flesh, Zen Bones*. Rutland, VT: Charles E. Tuttle, 1957.

Sekida, Katsuki. *Zen Training*. New York: John Weatherhill, 1975.

Suzuki, D. T. *Studies in Zen*. New York: Dell, 1955.

———— *Zen Buddhism*. New York: Doubleday, 1956.

———— *Mysticism: Christian and Buddhist*. London: Allen & Unwin, 1957.

Wei Tat. *Ch'eng Wei Shih Lun*. Hong Kong: The Ch'eng Wei Shih Lun Publishing Committee, 1973.

Zurcher, E. *The Buddhist Conquest of China*. Atlantic Highlands, NJ: Humanities Press, 1973.

Chinese Sources

Ch'an Hai (The Sea of Zen) (禪海), Nan Huai-chin, Lao Ku Publishing Co., Taipei, 1956.

Ch'an Men San Chu (Three Pillars of Zen; Kapleau) (禪門三柱), Ku Fa Yen (Tr.), Hui Chu Publishing Co., 1965.

Ch'an Te Hsun Lien (Zen Training; Sekida) (禪的訓練), Hsu Ching-fu (Tr.), T'ien Hua Publishing Co., Taipei, 1980.

Ch'an Tsung de Ts'ung Lin Chih Tu: (禪宗的叢林制度), Nan Huai-chin, Lao Ku Publishing Co., Taipei, 1959.

Ch'an Yu Tao Kai Lun (禪與道概論), Nan Huai-chin, Lao Ku Publishing Co., Taipei, 1968.

Ch'eng Wei Shih Lun (成唯識論), Hsuan-tsang (Tr.), T'ang Dynasty.

Chieh Shen Mi Ching (解深密經), Hsuan Tsang (Tr.), T'ang Dynasty.

Chih Yueh Lu (指月錄), Ch'u Ju-chi (Ed.), Sung Dynasty.

Chin Kang Ching (Diamond Sutra) (金剛經).

Ching Te Ch'uan Tung Lu (景德傳燈錄), Tao Yuan, Sung Dynasty.

Chuang Tze (莊子)

Chung Kuo Ch'an Tsung Shih Chuan (中國禪宗祖師傳), Taipei, 1967, Tseng P'u Hsin.

Chung Kuo Che Hsueh Chih Hsing (中國哲學思想), Ts'ang Kuang-en, Taipei, 1980.

Fa Hua Ching (法華經).

Fo Tzu Li Tai T'ung Tsai (佛祖歷代通載), Nien Ch'ang (Ed.), Yuan Dynasty.

Hsi Ch'an Lu Yin (習禪錄影), English title: *Profiles of Zen Training,* Nan Huai-chin, Lao Ku, Taipei, 1976.

Hua Yen Ching (華嚴經).

Huang Ti Nei Ching (黃帝內經), English title: *The Yellow Emperor's Internal Medicine Classic,* Han Dynasty.

Hsu Yun Ho Shang Nien P'u (虛雲和尚年譜), Lu Kuan Hsien, Taiwan Yin Ching Shu, 1958.

I Ching (易經), English title: *The Book of Change.*

Kao Seng Chuan (高僧傳)

Leng Yen Ching (楞嚴經).

Liao Fan Sse Hsun (了凡四訓), Yuan Liao Fan, Ming Dynasty.

Ling Yuan Ta Tao Ko Pai Hua Chu Chieh (靈源大道歌白話註解), Ts'ao Wen I, Sung Dynasty.

Lio Tzu T'an Ching (六祖壇經), English title: *The Altar Sutra of the Sixth Patriarch,* Hui Neng, T'ang Dynasty.

Lung Ch'ieh Ta Yi Chin Shih (楞伽大義今釋), Nan Huai-chin, Lao Ku, Taipei, 1965.

Lung Yen Ta Yi Chin Shih (楞嚴大義今釋), Nan Huai-chin, Lao Ku, Taipei, 1960.

Mi Le Jih Pa Tsun Che Chuan (密勒日巴尊者傳), Chang Ch'eng Chi, (Tr.), Hui Chu Publishing Co., Taipei, 1960.

P'ang Chu Shih Yu Lu (龐居士語錄), Chung Hua Fo Chiao Chu Shih Hui, Taipei, 1974.

Sse Shu (四書), English title: *The Four Books.*

Tao Te Ching (道德經), Lao Tze.

Ts'an Tung Ch'i Chih Chih (參同契直指), Wei Pai-yang, Han Dynasty.

Tsung Ching Lu (宗鏡錄), Yung Ming-shou, Sung Dynasty.

Wei Mo Ching She Ts'ung Shu (維摩精舍叢書), Yuan Huan Hsien (Ed.), Chengtu, Szechuan, 1943.

Wu Chen P'ien (悟真篇), Chang Tze Yang, Sung Dynasty.

Yung Chia Ch'an Tsung Chi (永嘉禪宗集), Yung Chia, Tang Dynasty.